W9-BCO-845

GLOBALVIEWPOINTS

Popular Culture

Other Books of Related Interest:

At Issue Series

Beauty Pageants

Does the Internet Increase Crime?

Is Childhood Becoming Too Sexualized?

Is Media Violence a Problem?

Global Viewpoints Series

The Culture of Beauty

The Internet

Introducing Issues with Opposing Viewpoints Series

Censorship

Gay Marriage

Globalization

Video Games

Opposing Viewpoints Series

Censorship

Consumerism

The Culture of Beauty

Globalization

Male and Female Roles

Mass Media

The Middle Class

Obesity

Popular Culture

Noah Berlatsky, Book Editor

GREENHAVEN PRESS
A part of Gale, Cengage Learning

Detroit • New York • San Francisco • New Haven, Conn • Waterville, Maine • London

GALE
CENGAGE Learning

Christine Nasso, *Publisher*
Elizabeth Des Chenes, *Managing Editor*

© 2011 Greenhaven Press, a part of Gale, Cengage Learning

Gale and Greenhaven Press are registered trademarks used herein under license.

For more information, contact:
Greenhaven Press
27500 Drake Rd.
Farmington Hills, MI 48331-3535
Or you can visit our Internet site at gale.cengage.com

For product information and technology assistance, contact us at

Gale Customer Support, 1-800-877-4253
For permission to use material from this text or product, submit all requests online at
www.cengage.com/permissions

Further permissions questions can be emailed to permissionrequest@cengage.com

Articles in Greenhaven Press anthologies are often edited for length to meet page requirements. In addition, original titles of these works are changed to clearly present the main thesis and to explicitly indicate the author's opinion. Every effort is made to ensure that Greenhaven Press accurately reflects the original intent of the authors. Every effort has been made to trace the owners of copyrighted material.

Cover image copyright © David Crausby/Alamy.

LIBRARY OF CONGRESS CATALOGING-IN-PUBLICATION DATA

Popular culture / Noah Berlatsky, book editor.
    p. cm. -- (Global viewpoints)
  Includes bibliographical references and index.
  ISBN 978-0-7377-5118-5 (hardcover) -- ISBN 978-0-7377-5119-2 (pbk.)
 1. Popular culture. I. Berlatsky, Noah.
 CB430.P628 2010
 306--dc22
                                                 2010019294

Printed in the United States of America

ACC LIBRARY SERVICES AUSTIN, TX

Contents

Chapter 2: Popular Culture and Intellectual Property Rights

Chapter 3: Popular Culture and Censorship

Satellite dishes, personal computers, and other technological advances have made it possible for many Iranians to experience Western music, film, and culture despite government bans. For similar reasons, Iranians are also increasingly able to make their own music and films.

National Socialist black metal (NSBM) deliberately espouses white supremacy. Mainstream companies who currently sell the music should stop.

Chapter 4: Popular Culture's Impact on Attitudes

The northeastern Isan region of Thailand has long been thought of in the country as an undesirable rural backwater. However, due to the success of the region's music in recent years, images of Isan have become much more positive.

Foreword

*"The problems of all of humanity can
only be solved by all of humanity."*
—*Swiss author Friedrich Dürrenmatt*

Global interdependence has become an undeniable reality.
Mass media and technology have increased worldwide
access to information and created a society of global citizens.
Understanding and navigating this global community is a
challenge, requiring a high degree of information literacy and
a new level of learning sophistication.

Building on the success of its flagship series, *Opposing
Viewpoints*, Greenhaven Press has created the *Global Viewpoints* series to examine a broad range of current, often controversial topics of worldwide importance from a variety of
international perspectives. Providing students and other readers with the information they need to explore global connec-
tions and think critically about worldwide implications, each
Global Viewpoints volume offers a panoramic view of a topic
of widespread significance.

Drugs, famine, immigration—a broad, international treat-
ment is essential to do justice to social, environmental, health,
and political issues such as these. Junior high, high school,
and early college students, as well as general readers, can all
use *Global Viewpoints* anthologies to discern the complexities
relating to each issue. Readers will be able to examine unique
national perspectives while, at the same time, appreciating the
interconnectedness that global priorities bring to all nations
and cultures.

Material in each volume is selected from a diverse range of
sources, including journals, magazines, newspapers, nonfiction
books, speeches, government documents, pamphlets, organiza-

tion newsletters, and position papers. *Global Viewpoints* is truly global, with material drawn primarily from international sources available in English and secondarily from U.S. sources with extensive international coverage.

Features of each volume in the *Global Viewpoints* series include:

- An **annotated table of contents** that provides a brief summary of each essay in the volume, including the name of the country or area covered in the essay.

- An **introduction** specific to the volume topic.

- A **world map** to help readers locate the countries or areas covered in the essays.

- For each viewpoint, an **introduction** that contains notes about the author and source of the viewpoint explains why material from the specific country is being presented, summarizes the main points of the viewpoint, and offers three **guided reading questions** to aid in understanding and comprehension.

- **For further discussion** questions that promote critical thinking by asking the reader to compare and contrast aspects of the viewpoints or draw conclusions about perspectives and arguments.

- A worldwide list of **organizations to contact** for readers seeking additional information.

- A **periodical bibliography** for each chapter and a **bibliography of books** on the volume topic to aid in further research.

- A comprehensive **subject index** to offer access to people, places, events, and subjects cited in the text, with the countries covered in the viewpoints highlighted.

Global Viewpoints is designed for a broad spectrum of readers who want to learn more about current events, history, political science, government, international relations, economics, environmental science, world cultures, and sociology—students doing research for class assignments or debates, teachers and faculty seeking to supplement course materials, and others wanting to understand current issues better. By presenting how people in various countries perceive the root causes, current consequences, and proposed solutions to worldwide challenges, *Global Viewpoints* volumes offer readers opportunities to enhance their global awareness and their knowledge of cultures worldwide.

Introduction

"Even if I had any money I would rather burn everything I own and not even give them the ashes. They could have the job of picking them up. That's how much I hate the media industry."

Peter Sunde Kolmisoppi,
founder of the file sharing Web site
the Pirate Bay, upon being ordered
by a court to pay damages
to copyright holders

The Internet has had an enormous impact on the distribution of popular culture around the world. Today a huge quantity of free movies, video games, music, comic books, and books are downloadable online over the Web. In some cases, these items are available for sale through legitimate sellers, who have agreements with the creators. Many times, though, copyrighted materials are distributed for free, without the permission of and with no payment going to the copyright holders.

One of the most successful free content sites is the Pirate Bay (TPB). The Pirate Bay was launched in 2003 as a project of Piratbyrán, a Swedish think tank devoted to the promotion of free culture and the loosening of copyright restrictions and intellectual property regulations. In 2004 TPB separated from Piratbyrán and continued as a commercial endeavor.

The Pirate Bay was designed to allow large numbers of users to share files for free. The Pirate Bay uses a technology called BitTorrent. What this means is that TPB "does not itself host audio and video files," according to Kevin Anderson in an April 17, 2009, article in the *Guardian*. Instead, TPB users store files on their own hard drives. Users then use a torrent file to connect to the network and share material. To find that torrent file with the content they want, though, users need a link, "like the index card in a library catalog," according to Flora Graham in a February 16, 2009, article on the BBC News Web site. The Pirate Bay provides a catalog of these links, connecting users to each other.

Because it has no copyrighted material on its own server, and because it is based in Sweden where intellectual property laws are relatively lax, the Pirate Bay has felt confident in defying cease and desist orders from copyright holders. For instance, in 2004 the film production company DreamWorks Pictures demanded that TPB remove links to *Shrek 2*. The Pirate Bay posted the cease and desist letter on its site along with an insulting response dated August 23, 2004. In the response, TPB called DreamWorks and its lawyers "morons" and claimed that "Sweden is not a state in the United States of America. . . . US law does not apply here."

Over time a number of other file sharing services were shut down or forced to remove content, but TPB continued to defy copyright holders. By 2007, the site had 5 million active users and was the 292nd most popular site in the world, beating out the U.S. Postal Service and Wal-Mart, according to David Sarno writing on April 29, 2007, in the *Los Angeles Times*. The same article noted that, according to the Motion Picture Association of America (MPAA), the motion picture industry alone "lost more than $7 billion as a result of Internet piracy" in 2005.

As perhaps the most visible file sharing site, however, TPB has attracted legal challenges. In 2006 the Swedish government, possibly in consultation with the Motion Picture Association (the international branch of the MPAA), raided the offices of the Pirate Bay, seizing file servers and holding two of TPB administrators, Gottfrid Svartholm Warg and Fredrik Neij, for questioning, according to Flora Graham in the BBC News article.

The raid did not shut down TPB; instead, a network of servers was set up so that shutting down one location would only close the site for minutes. However, media companies such as Warner Bros. and Columbia Pictures continued to pursue legal action in Swedish court against Warg, Neij, and the two other administrators of the Pirate Bay, Carl Lundström and Peter Sunde Kolmisoppi. The prosecution accused the four of "assisting copyright infringement," according to a January 31, 2008, article on TorrentFreak, a blog that reports news related to BitTorrent and file sharing. The prosecution also insisted that TPB profited from copyright violation by placing ads on the site. The prosecution said that these ads generate more than $3 million a year.

In 2009, TPB administrators were found guilty of breaking copyright law. They were sentenced to a year in jail and ordered to pay $4.5 million in damages. John Kennedy, the chairman of the International Federation of the Phonographic Industry, said, "There has been a perception that piracy is OK and that the music industry should just have to accept it. This verdict will change that," as quoted in an April 17, 2009, BBC News article.

Other commenters, however, were not so sure that the TPB verdict would cause a major change in file sharing. The Pirate Bay has appealed the ruling and hopes to gain a reversal in a higher court. Moreover, as of April 2010, a year after the ruling, TPB was continuing to operate. Writing at *PC-World* on April 17, 2009, JR Raphael noted "even if the Pirate Bay itself were somehow to be shuttered, there are countless other comparable tracking services all over the world. Could they all be targeted and taken down? It's highly unlikely." Christian Engström, a European Parliament candidate of Sweden's Pirate Party—a political party devoted to loosening copyright restrictions—was also skeptical about the long-term effects of the verdict. If companies "think they're going to make people stop file sharing then they're living in a fantasy world," he said, as quoted by Kelly Fiveash in an April 17, 2009, article on the Register Web site.

The Pirate Bay case suggests a number of important controversies surrounding popular culture today. The viewpoints in this book will look at other issues in chapters including Popular Culture and Globalization, Popular Culture and Intellectual Property Rights, Popular Culture and Censorship, and Popular Culture's Impact on Attitudes. The authors of the viewpoints in this volume will examine the ways in which the distribution, content, ownership, and availability of popular culture affect people throughout the world.

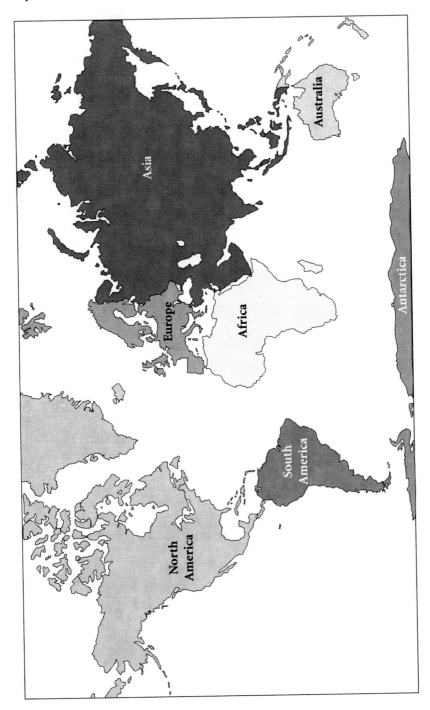

GLOBALVIEWPOINTS

Popular Culture and Globalization

Globalization of Pop Culture Does Not Reduce Real Differences

Louis de Lamare

Louis de Lamare is a writer whose work has appeared on Montray Kréyol, a French-West Indian creole language resource Web site. In the following viewpoint, he argues that even though America's cultural products are exported throughout the world, they do not reduce real differences worldwide. On the contrary, America's widespread power and influence may increase resentments and conflicts. He concludes that deep divisions between haves and have-nots remain, and may even be exacerbated by globalization.

As you read, consider the following questions:

1. According to de Lamare, what percentage of software, recorded music, and books come from the United States?

2. What does Samuel P. Huntington believe the world is headed toward?

3. Why does the author say that many intellectuals disdain popular culture?

Louis de Lamare, "Cultural Globalisation: What Is It?" *Montray Kréyol*, May 5, 2009. Reproduced by permission.

Globalisation has been the buzz word since the early nineties so much that the term "globalisation" has become somewhat like a cliché to explain everything that is new and manifesting in this iron age of rapid communication and technological progress.

Cultural Globalisation

While we can now distinguish the various faces of globalisation i.e., the economic, cultural, political and military, academics like Robert Keohane and Joseph Nye Jr. remind us that ... the social and cultural globalisation "involves the movement of ideas, information, images and people." In trying to define cultural globalisation, it is probably more relevant that we first try to understand how cultural globalisation works and affects our lives and consequently see whether it is unifying or rather a subject of discord that tends to separate or segregate communities of people.

While it is acknowledged that culture is probably one of the most complicated words in the English language, it is probably due to the dynamics of culture i.e., it was never meant to be static. The notion of culture has gone a long way from the traditional definition to embrace new and emerging trends, new ideas and new ways of how people behave in the light of progress and modernism.

From the anthropological context, culture is more indigenous and refers to elements that condition and distinguishes human life as opposed to other mammals and gives a sense of identity. The main ingredients are probably language, history, religion, customs, artifacts, cooking, values, traditions, and also dependent upon man's capacity for learning and transmitting knowledge to succeeding generations. While some societies have shut themselves up and try to protect [themselves] from external influence (corruption) to preserve their culture, others are more open by allowing the dynamics of interaction to play or again by reaching out. For example many countries today are multicultural and multiculturalism is seen more of an enrichment than a threat by these societies.

On the other hand we are witnessing a new modern wave emerging from the West, not to say from America, which is defined as popular culture and which is flourishing. With the help of modern technology and communication, it transcends borders easily and even reaches rich and poor countries, young and old, east or west, north or south and makes no distinction at all on its way. E.g., My mother who is nearly 80 years old and can hardly speak English watches CNN and likes the American movies and soaps as well as American talk-back TV. She is not an exception as these TV shows are as popular in the rich as well as in the poor countries, in Asia as well as in Africa. The youth of the world listen and dance the latest American hip-hop. The fast-food chains or the McWorld are common features even in traditional societies like India. We can cite many examples where the Western lifestyle, be it wearing Levi's jeans, using cellular phones, using the English language are becoming more and more popular in developed or newly developed world, as well as in the third world countries. These are probably the most obvious signs that support ... the convergence theory. We are all becoming the same and in so doing we are embracing a global culture.

The Rise of Popular Culture

The rise of popular culture is no coincidence as it is tributary to the economic globalisation. David Rothkopf [president and CEO of Garten Rothkopf, an international advisory firm] makes no apology when he says that it is in the best interest of America that we all converge to the same cultural way. He argues that cultural differences lead to conflicts and even genocides; he cites examples of ethnic conflicts and conflict between cultural cousins, e.g., Cambodia, Bosnia and Rwanda, Sudan and Algeria. [All of these sites have witnessed serious ethnic violence and/or genocides in the last 50 years.] He goes on by describing how "the decline of cultural distinction may be a measure for progress of civilization, a tangible sign of enhanced communication and understanding."

It is a fact that the United States dominates the global traffic in information and ideas and as statistics show: 75% of the prepackaged software, 60% of prerecorded music, 32% of books come from America. . . . So behind this use of soft power, there is also the huge economic benefit as well as political benefit for America, not only in terms of exporting its products but marketing the American model and acceptance of its values which lies in democracy, free trade, individual freedom, and capitalism. Again as David Rothkopf writes, "America should not shy away from doing what is so clearly in their economic, political and security interest" by promoting its values which he describes "as the most tolerant, the most willing to constantly reassess and improve itself and the best model for the future".

It is a fact that the United States dominates the global traffic in information and ideas.

Now that we have seen cultural globalisation at work, it is time to asses its impact.

[American political scientist] Samuel [P.] Huntington well before September 11[, 2001, when terrorists attacked the United States] was saying that the world was heading towards a clash of civilizations. He based his arguments in the realists' theory that nation states will not decline and instead the principal conflicts of global politics will occur between nations and groups of different civilizations. His predictions lie in the empirical observation of how the world is fragmented in terms of culture and civilization. His arguments also rest on the facts that:

1. Differences among civilization are basic.

2. The growing interaction among people intensifies civilization consciousness.

3. The economic modernization and social change are separating people from local identities.

4. The growth of civilization-consciousness is enhanced by the West and that a de-Westernization and indigenization of elites is occurring in many non-Western countries.

5. Even more than ethnicity, religion discriminates sharply and exclusively among people.

6. Successful economic regionalism will reinforce civilization consciousness.

Conflicts Have Not Ended

Again it cannot be denied that despite the use of strong geopolitics and the use of soft power, conflicts have not stopped. However while there is less war among nations there has been increasing wars, antagonism and rivalry based on cultural or ethnic differences. We can cite examples like Israelites-Palestinians, Sunnis against Shia in Iraq, Muslims and Serbians in the Balkans, in Sudan, in Indonesia, in the Philippines, in Russia, in the Middle East, Iran-Iraq, Lebanon-Syria and Iraq-Kuwait, the rise of Islamist fundamentalism and terrorism are many reasons that support Huntington's prediction. However there are many critics of Huntington's piece of analysis and they come mainly from liberalist institutionalists supporting that war is becoming more and more irrelevant and too costly for nation states. It is also observed that today people are more preoccupied with trade, modernism, and want to become more affluent and improve their lot. The tendency is towards a consumer society and embracing the capitalist model of production and profit. Values of freedom and democracy are taking over. It is obvious that each and every-

The Clash of Civilizations

Because of all of the momentous changes in communications and transportation, people from different civilizations are interacting in a way they haven't before, and are interacting on a more equal basis. . . .

We have a world in which there are a significant number of major civilizations—it's a pluralistic world. And while the United States is undoubtedly more powerful than other countries, it's not terribly useful to think of it roughly, or even primarily, in terms of a hierarchical world. The United States, as well as the European Union, Japan and other major actors all have to take into consideration the interests and probable responses of other major actors to what they do. I think religion certainly plays a tremendously important role. It is manifest broadly, but not exclusively, in the rise of religious consciousness in the Muslim world.

Samuel P. Huntington, as told to Mark O'Keefe,
"Five Years After 9/11, the Clash of Civilizations Revisited,"
Pew Forum on Religion & Public Life, August 18, 2006.
www.pewforum.org.

one is looking positively or aspiring to be part of the elite; the Davos [Switzerland, home of the World Economic Forum] culture club. The blatant fact is also that this popular culture makes it all easy for people, especially the young generation to relate to each other. The easiness of long-distance communication with technological progress makes the world like a global village. The impact of popular global culture cannot be minimized as it plays a very important role in that new ideology and mode of thinking or behaving.

While there seems to be a lot on the surface to conclude that "we are all the same", but is it really the case? Is it because the youth of the Middle East wear jeans that they have turned down their faith, religion or culture and suddenly become disrespectful towards their elders? Is it because the French youngsters watch more American movies that the French language or culture is regressing? Is it because most of the Asians are studying or have been educated in Western universities that there is no more an "Asian way" as advocated by Mahathir Mohamad [a Malaysian political leader who criticized globalisation] and Lee Kwan-Yew [a political leader in Singapore]?

It cannot be denied that despite the use of strong geopolitics and the use of soft power, conflicts have not stopped.

When we scratch the surface, the reality could be completely different. In a study conducted by the United [Nations] Development Programme in 2003 on quality of life, USA ranked behind Norway, Iceland, Sweden, Australia, the Netherlands and Belgium and that France and Spain attract more tourists than the United States. The same report shows that in the run-up to the Iraq war [when the U.S. invaded Iraq in 2003] ... [there was increasing] anti-American sentiment. According to [political theorist] Joseph Nye Jr., "Another source of anti-Americanism is structural. The US is the big kid on the block and the disproportion in power engenders a mixture of admiration, envy and resentment."

The resentment is manifested in many ways, Max Weber, the English sociologist, claims that there is a renaissance of local culture and language in reaction to the assault against it by Western culture ... [which] is an arrogant ... secular, revolutionary ideology and a mask of US hegemony. The fragmentation is also manifested in covert and overt forms, through academic debates and through public manifestations. Edward Said in his book *Orientalism* criticizes the West for a narrow view of the Orient and how ... there is a growing concern among intellectuals and locals that this global culture poses a threat to the sovereignty and territoriality of their homeland and ... that popular culture seduces through sheer force of marketing and promise of pleasure which is more immediate than long term. Many intellectuals disdain popular culture because of its crude commercialism and gearing more towards a consumer society rather that a production one. There is thus a fear of destruction of traditional values by corruption.... The resentment of the cultural domination elite, according to Samuel [P.] Huntington, may also lead to the emergence of nationalist and religious counter elite.

While millions are leading a hand-to-mouth existence it is hard to conceive how they can aspire to converge to a global culture while living in a different reality.

Haves and Have-Nots

Asking the question of whether cultural globalisation makes people more the same or different, [political theorist] J.A. Scholte found that while it introduces a single world culture centered on consumerism, mass media, America and the English language, other diagnoses have linked it to enduring or even increasing cultural diversity. She opines that globalisation has not kept countless people from continuing to embrace national differences. While it can be true, to some extent, that the American economic and cultural attraction has won over the hearts and minds of the majorities of the young people of the Western world, it cannot be said with the same certainty that it is the case in the other parts of the world. We have to consider that today millions of Africans live in absolute poverty, that fundamentalism and extremism are on the rise, that most Asian countries are still entrenched in their traditional culture, that most of the islands of the Indian Ocean, the Caribbean and the Pacific still have strong feelings about their heritage. While millions are leading a hand-to-mouth existence it is hard to conceive how they can aspire to converge to a global culture while living in a different reality. The rise of the popular culture is having more impact in Western countries where paradoxically, more debates and questions are raised mainly by academics. As a matter of fact, cultural globalisation has less effect in Asia, Russia, India, China, Africa and the Middle East. While it is touching those who can afford it because it also comes with a price, most of the rest seem to be out of it. So it can be said that popular culture is rather making a clear distinction and division among who is in and who is out, just like the economic globalisation is causing a bigger gap between the haves and the haves-not.

The question of a global culture and its ramifications will surely continue to be an everlasting debate of whether it is unifying or rather dividing.

Venezuela Enacted Laws to Make Its Music More Local and Diverse

Monte Reel

Monte Reel is a reporter for the Washington Post. *In the following viewpoint, he reports that the Venezuelan government introduced a law requiring that 50 percent of the music played on the radio be Venezuelan. With additional radio exposure, traditional Venezuelan performers have seen their record sales surge, Reel says. Though international groups and musicians are unhappy with the law, Reel found that many Venezuelans seemed pleased at the increased diversity of music on the radio.*

As you read, consider the following questions:

1. According to the manager of the Disco Center Superstore, how much of his business comes from traditional Venezuelan artists since the passage of the new law regulating radio content?
2. After the passage of the new law, what kind of increase did Venezuela's Traditional National Orchestra see in its CD sales?
3. What group does Reel say opposes the new law?

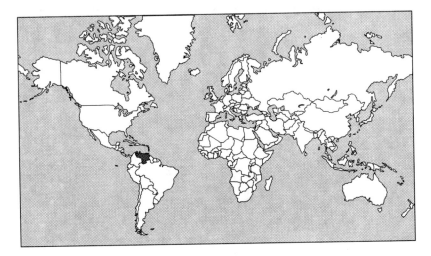

If [American pop singer] Britney Spears & Co. aren't selling as many records here [in Caracas, Venezuela] as they used to, they should point their fingers at a man who would be thrilled to shoulder the blame: [Venezuelan] President Hugo Chávez.

Promoting Music by Law

The National Assembly, which is dominated by Chávez, recently passed a law requiring that no less than 50 percent of all music played on the nation's radio stations be Venezuelan. Of that, half must be classified as "traditional," showcasing . . . "the presence of traditional Venezuelan values." Chávez backers say the harps and *bandolas* [a small, pear-shaped, guitarlike instrument] that now resound through this country of 25 million are playing the overture to a musical revolution.

"We've always had traditional Venezuelan records in stock, but before a few months ago we never sold any—not one," said Miguel Angel Guada, manager of the Disco Center Superstore in one of the capital's largest malls. "It was all Britney Spears, Backstreet Boys [an American pop group] and that sort of thing. But now I'd say one-third of our business comes from Venezuelan artists, which is absolutely incredible."

The new law can make listening to the radio an adventure in dizzying contrasts. One minute a disc jockey might spin Puerto Rico's Daddy Yankee rapping about "Biggie and Pac," [referring to American rappers Biggie Smalls and Tupac Shakur] and the next minute it's flutes and fiddles from the Andean highlands. Some Venezuelan rock and pop artists have begun to record cover versions of traditional songs to take advantage of the mandates. Almost all local artists, regardless of age or genre, are reaping the rewards.

The new law can make listening to the radio an adventure in dizzying contrasts.

Traditional Musicians Reap Benefits

Members of Venezuela's Traditional National Orchestra used to lament how their compact discs would languish on vending tables at their concerts, but this year [2005] they watched sales take off with whiplash force—from zero to 200 copies sold at a single performance. The orchestra is using the extra income to record more albums, according to Sigfrido Chiva, its president.

"After the law was approved and the music started being played on the radio, I began getting telephone calls to go on talk shows—maybe 10 or 15 of them in the last couple of months," said Chiva, a violinist. "In my 52 years as a musician before that, I had never gotten a single call."

Radio listeners say they occasionally detect muted grumblings from pop and hip-hop DJs when they introduce the songs that meet the law's requirements. But a casual survey at Caracas record stores suggested that many Venezuelans are enjoying the variety.

"It's kind of the fashion now to listen to traditional music," said Rafael Quintero, 19. "It has just taken off in the last three months."

Jesus Alallon, 42, said he liked the new radio playlists, which he credits for changing his music-buying habits. "I buy more traditional music now," he said. "If I buy 10 records, I'd say one of them is probably traditional."

The Venezuelan government enacted similar radio guidelines in the 1980s to support the local music industry, but the rules did not have legal teeth and were widely interpreted as mere suggestions. After the 1990s, free market economics reigned, and Venezuelan music—particularly its traditional forms—all but disappeared. Record companies produced fewer traditional albums, and the lack of them is becoming painfully obvious to some listeners.

A casual survey at Caracas record stores suggested that many Venezuelans are enjoying the variety.

"I am a little concerned that the quality of some of the national music being broadcast isn't very high," said Eduardo Ramirez, who plays mandolin and *cuatro*, a four-string guitar, for the Traditional National Orchestra. "Some of the versions are of such low quality that I'm afraid they distort the original compositions. There's a revival of older recordings now, mainly because there's not enough material to fill all of the airtime."

The recording industry outside Venezuela, not surprisingly, isn't fond of the radio mandates. The International Intellectual Property Alliance, a private-sector coalition that represents U.S. copyright-based industries, reported that the new radio regulations and high piracy rates have combined to create "the bleakest scenario the industry has faced in its history" in Venezuela.

The new law "represents a serious commercial barrier to all international music by limiting its exposure to consumers and restricting the potential revenues it can generate through broadcasting fees," the organization stated in a report this year.

But to many Venezuelans, America's loss is their country's gain. Gustavo Arroyo, 20, dreams of being a singer in a successful band. For two years, he and his friends have been performing at parties, playing a mix of contemporary and traditional music. Even though one of his friends recently moved to Mexico, Arroyo said the band's dreams have not died. The new law, he added, doesn't hurt their chances.

In India, Globalization Creates Growth of Popular Religiosity

William Dalrymple

William Dalrymple is the New Statesman's *south Asia correspondent. His most recent book is* Nine Lives: In Search of the Sacred in Modern India. *In the following viewpoint, he discusses the trend of growing spirituality in India, a movement away from the secularism of the past few generations. Not only is there a growth in the patronage of local shrines, but Hinduism has become a focal point of local and national politics. As a result, the wide variety of local beliefs that Hinduism embraced in the past is being overtaken by a more monolithic religion espoused by the Indian urban middle class.*

As you read, consider the following questions:

1. According to the author, what leader was repsonsible for secularizing India?
2. What is "karma capitalism"?
3. What is the RSS?

Globalisation has been good for gods in the Indian subcontinent. As the region has remade itself, it has grown more devout, and its religions are becoming ever more entangled with politics.

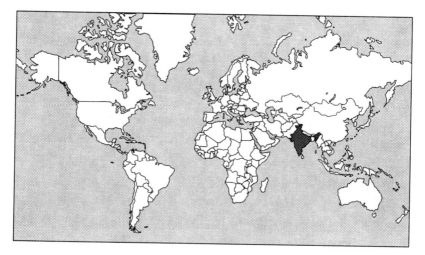

Growth of the Cult of Om Singh

On a foggy winter's night in November 1998, Om Singh, a young landowner from Rajasthan, was riding his Enfield Bullet back home after winning a local election near Jodhpur, when he misjudged a turning and hit a tree. He was killed instantly. As a memorial, his father fixed the motorbike to a stand, raised on a concrete plinth under the shelter of a small canopy, near the site of the crash.

"We were a little surprised when people started reporting miracles near the bike," Om's uncle Shaitan Singh told me on my last visit. "Om was no saint, and people say he had had a drink or two before his crash. In fact, there was no indication whatsoever during his life that he was a deity. He just loved his horses and his motorbike. But since his death a lot of people have had their wishes fulfilled here—particularly women who want children. For them, he has become very powerful. They sit on the bike, make offerings to Om Singh-ji, and it is said that flowers drop into their laps. Nine months later they have sons. Every day people see him. He comes to many people in their dreams."

"How did it all begin?" I asked. We were in the middle of a surging throng: crowds of red-turbaned and brightly sari-ed villagers gathered around the bike, the women queuing patiently to straddle its seat and ring the bell on the canopy. Nearby, two drummers were loudly banging dholaks [Indian hand drums], while chai-shop owners made tea and paan for the pilgrims. Other stalls sold plaques, postcards and statues of Om Singh and his motorbike. Pieces of cloth were tied to branches all over the tree and gold flags flapped in the desert wind. Everywhere buses and trucks were disgorging pilgrims coming to visit Rajasthan's newest shrine.

"First it was just family and friends who came," Shaitan Singh replied. "Then people realised there was a certain power here. It wasn't just the Hindus: Muslims came, too. Now the truck drivers will never pass this spot without stopping and making an offering. Every year the crowd grows."

"Do you believe in Om's power?" I asked.

"The more faith grows," he answered enigmatically, "the stronger it becomes."

India Moves Away from Secularism

Across the subcontinent, faith has been growing and religion becoming stronger as the region develops and reinvents itself. In 19th-century Europe, industrialisation and the mass migrations from farms and villages to the towns and cities went hand in hand with the Death of God: organised religion began to decline, and the church and state moved further and further apart. The experience of south Asia has been more or less the reverse of this.

During the early 20th century, educated, urban Hindu reformers moved away from ritualised expressions of faith, and early leaders such as Jawaharlal Nehru and BR Ambedkar constitutionally formed India as a model secular state with no official faith: This was to be a nation where, in the words of Nehru, dams would be the new temples. But over the past 20 years, just as India has freed itself from the shackles of Nehruvian socialism, so India has also gone a long way to try to shake off Nehruvian secularism, too. The revival of religiosity and religious extremism in Pakistan may be more the focus of the international media, especially as Barack Obama grapples in vain with the troubled region now hyphenated as Af-Pak, but what is happening in India is equally remarkable and in many ways surprisingly similar.

The dramatic revival of piety and religion in India has recently been the subject of a remarkable study by Meera Nanda, a Delhi-based academic who has shown how globalisation may be making India richer, and arguably more materialistic, but it is also making Indians more religious, and at the same time making religion more political. "Globalisation has been good for the gods," she writes in *The God Market*.

> But over the past 20 years, just as India has freed itself from the shackles of Nehruvian socialism, so India has also gone a long way to try to shake off Nehruvian secularism, too.

As India is liberalising and globalising its economy, the country is experiencing a rising tide of popular Hinduism which is leaving no social segment and no public institution untouched. There is a surge in popular religiosity among the burgeoning and largely Hindu middle classes, as is evident from a boom in pilgrimage and the invention of new, more ostentatious rituals. This religiosity is being cultivated by the emerging state-temple-corporate complex that is replacing the more secular public institutions of the Nehruvian era ... a new Hindu religiosity is getting more deeply embedded in everyday life, in both the private and public spheres.

India now has 2.5 million places of worship, but only 1.5 million schools and barely 75,000 hospitals. Pilgrimages account for more than 50 per cent of all package tours, the bigger pilgrimage sites now vying with the Taj Mahal for the most visited sites in the country: the Balaji Temple in Tirupati had 23 million visitors in 2008, while over 17 million trekked to the mountain shrine of Vaishno Devi.

In a 2007 survey jointly conducted by the *Hindustan Times* and the CNN-IBN news channel, 30 per cent of Indians said they had become more religious in the past five years. Such is the appetite for rituals in this newly religious middle class that there has recently been a severe shortfall of English- and Sanskrit-speaking priests with the qualifications to perform Vedic and Agamic rites. When it comes to rituals in the new India, demand has completely outstripped supply.

In her book, Nanda writes engagingly about what she calls "karma capitalism" and the Indian equivalent of American tel-evangelists, the TV God Men, some of whom have huge followings: Sri Sri Ravi Shankar, who is in many ways India's Pat Robertson, has built a global spirituality empire called the Art of Living, which claims 20 million members, and much of whose land has been donated by Indian state governments.

The Interaction of Religion and Politics

Meanwhile, religion and politics are becoming ever more entangled. Nanda presents interesting evidence about the dramatic increase in state funding for yagnas (fire sacrifices), yoga camps and temple tourism, as well as the sharp increase in state donation of land for temples, ashrams and training schools for temple priests. In Rajasthan, the government annually spends 260 million rupees on temple renovations and training for Hindu priests. Mass pujas (prayers) and public yagnas have become an important part of political campaigning for all parties, not just the overtly Hindu Bharatiya Janata Party (BJP).

Perhaps surprisingly, India's growing band of techies and software professionals seems particularly open both to religiosity in general and to hard right-wing Hindu nationalism in particular, so much so that many have joined a special wing of the far-right Rashtriya Swayamsevak Sangh (the National Association of Volunteers), the organisation to which Mahatma Gandhi's assassin belonged. The RSS now organises regular social meetings called IT-milans, where right-wing techies can "meet like-minded people and get a sense of participating in something bigger than just punching keyboards all day".

The modernisation of the RSS is certainly one of the more worrying trends in Indian religiosity, as is the organisation's increasing respectability in the eyes of the urban Indian middle class. For, like the Phalange in Lebanon, the RSS was founded in direct imitation of European fascist movements. Like its 1930s models, it still makes much of daily parading in khaki drill and the giving of militaristic salutes (the RSS salute differs from that of the Nazis only in the angle of the forearm, which is held horizontally over the chest). The idea is to create a corps of dedicated paramilitary zealots who will bring about a revival of what the RSS sees as the lost Hindu golden age of national strength and purity.

Finally, at a rally in December 1992, a crowd of 200,000 militants, whipped into a frenzy by inflammatory BJP statements, stormed the barricades. Shouting "Death to the Muslims!" they attacked the mosque [in the town of Ayodhya] with sledgehammers.

The BJP, which governed India from 1999 until 2004, and is now the principal opposition party, was founded as the political wing of the RSS, and most senior BJP figures hold posts in both organisations. Though the BJP is certainly much more moderate and pragmatic than the RSS—like Likud in Israel, the BJP is a party that embraces a wide spectrum of right-wing opinion, ranging from mildly conservative free marketeers to raving ultra-nationalists—both organisations believe, as the centrepiece of their ideology, that India is in essence a Hindu nation and that the minorities may live in India only if they acknowledge this.

The most notable political manifestation of the increasing presence of religion in Indian life took place in the early 1990s as the Hindu right rose slowly to power, partly as a result of taking advantage of a long-running dispute over a small mosque in the northern Indian town of Ayodhya. The argument revolved around the question of whether Mir Baqi, a general of the Mughal emperor Babur (1483-1530), had built the mosque over a temple commemorating the birthplace of the Hindu god Lord Ram.

Although there was no evidence to confirm the existence of the temple or even to identify the modern town of Ayodhya with its legendary predecessor, Hindu organisations began holding rallies at the site, campaigning for the rebuilding of the temple. Finally, at a rally in December 1992, a crowd of 200,000 militants, whipped into a frenzy by inflammatory BJP statements, stormed the barricades. Shouting "Death to the Muslims!" they attacked the mosque with sledgehammers. One after another, like symbols of India's traditions of tolerance, democracy and secularism, the three domes were smashed to rubble.

Over the next month, violent unrest swept India: Mobs went on the rampage and Muslims were burned alive in their homes, scalded by acid bombs or knifed in the street. By the time the army was brought in, at least 1,400 people had been slaughtered in Bombay alone. It was a measure of how polarised things had become in India that this violence played so well with the electorate. In 1991, the BJP had taken 113 seats in parliament, up from 89 in the previous election. In 1996 that proportion virtually doubled, and the BJP became the largest party. After the 1999 general election, with 179 seats, it was finally able to take the reins of power into its hands.

Since then, however, the BJP has lost two general elections, largely for economic reasons, and perhaps especially their neglect of India's farmers; the ability of the religious right to mobilise votes by exploiting communal religious grievances seems, thankfully, to have diminished. But as large-scale anti-Christian riots in Orissa last year [2008] showed, it doesn't take much to wake the sleeping dragon of communal conflict from its slumber, and Ayodhya remains an emotive and divisive issue. If religion is no longer a vote-winner for the BJP, it is largely because other parties have found more subtle ways to use its ever-growing power.

The Homogenisation of Hinduism

For the growing politicisation of faith among the middle classes is only part of a much wider story. Behind the headlines, and beyond the political sphere, in the small towns and villages suspended between modernity and tradition, Indian religion is in a state of fascinating flux. Over the past couple of years, while researching *Nine Lives*, my book on local and folk beliefs in contemporary India, I have been very struck by how fast forms of traditional Indian devotion have been changing, even in the villages and backwaters, as India transforms itself at breakneck speed.

As is now well known, India is already on the verge of overtaking Japan to become the third-largest economy in the world; the Indian economy is expected to overtake that of the United States by roughly 2050. Much has now been written about the way that India is moving forward to return the subcontinent to its historical place at the heart of global trade, but so far little has been said about the way these huge earthquakes have affected the diverse religious traditions of south Asia, and particularly the archaic and deeply embedded syncretic, pluralist folk traditions that continue to defy the artificial boundaries of modern political identities.

Though the West often likes to imagine the religions of the East as deep wells of ancient and unchanging wisdom, in reality much of India's religious identity is closely tied to specific social groups, caste practices and father-to-son lineages, all of which are changing rapidly as Indian society transforms itself beyond recognition.

Certainly on my travels around India for *Nine Lives*, I found many worlds strangely colliding as the velocity of this process increases. In Jaipur, I spent time with Mohan Bhopa, an illiterate goatherd from Rajasthan who keeps alive a 4,000-line sacred epic that he, now virtually alone, still knows by heart. Living as a wandering bard and storyteller, he remembers the slokas of one of the great oral epics of Rajasthan praising the hero-god Papuji. Mohan told me, however, that his ancient recitative art is threatened by the lure of Bollywood and the Hindu epics shown on Indian TV, and he has had to adapt the old bardic tradition in order to survive.

The epic that Mohan recites contains a regional variant on the "national" Ramayana myth. In the main Ramayana tradition, the hero Lord Ram goes to Lanka to rescue his wife, Sita, who has been captured by the demon king Ravana. In the Rajasthani version of the myth, the hero is Papuji, and he goes to Lanka, not to rescue a kidnapped spouse, but to rustle Ravana's camels. It is exactly these sorts of regional variants, and self-contained local cults, which are being lost and menaced by what the eminent Indian historian Romila Thapar calls the new "syndicated Hinduism".

. . . Hinduism has slowly become systemised into a relatively centralised nationalist ideology which now increasingly resembles the very different structures of the Semitic belief systems that its more extreme adherents tend to abhor.

As Thapar explains in a celebrated essay on the subject, Hinduism is different from other major world religions in that it has no founder and no founding text. Indeed, the idea that Hinduism constitutes a single system is a very recent idea, dating from the arrival of the British in Bengal in the 18th century. Used to Western systems of faith, early colonial scholars organised many of the disparate, overlapping multi-

plicity of non-Abrahamic religious practices, cults, myths, festivals and rival deities that they encountered across south Asia
into a new world religion that they described as "Hinduism".

Since the mid-19th century, Hindu reformers such as
[Swami] Vivekananda have taken this process forward, so that
Hinduism has slowly become systemised into a relatively centralised nationalist ideology which now increasingly resembles
the very different structures of the Semitic belief systems that
its more extreme adherents tend to abhor. "The model," writes
Thapar, "is in fact that of Islam and Christianity . . . worship
is increasingly congregational and the introduction of ser-
mons on the definition of a good Hindu and Hindu belief
and behaviour [is] becoming common, and register[s] a dis-
tinct change from earlier practice."

According to Thapar, the speed of this homogenising process is now rising. "The emergence of a powerful middle class",
she believes, has created a desire for a "uniform, monolithic
Hinduism, created to serve its new requirements". This Hinduism masquerades as the revival of something ancient and traditional, but it is really "a new creation, created to support the
claims of [Hindu] majoritarianism".

All over India, villages were once believed to be host to a
numberless pantheon of sprites and godlings, tree spirits and
snake gods who were said to guard and regulate the ebb and
flow of daily life. They were worshipped and propitiated, as
they knew the till and soil of the local fields and the sweet wa-
ter of the wells, even the needs and thirsts of the cattle and
the goats in the village. But increasingly in urban India, these
small gods and goddesses are falling away and out of favour as
faith becomes more centralised, and as local gods and goddesses give way to the national, hyper-masculine hero deities,
especially Lord Krishna and Lord Ram, a process that scholars
call the "Rama-fication" of Hinduism. New deities are emerging, but carefully tailored for satisfying modern and middle-
class needs, such as Santoshi Maa, who first reached national

43

consciousness in the 1970's Bollywood film *Jai Santoshi Maa.* Also popular are other new deities such as Shani Maharaj, who neutralises the negative impact of the planet Saturn, and AIDS Amma, who reputedly has the power to do away with HIV.

Australian Popular Culture Is Diminished by Americanization

Andrew Guild

Andrew Guild writes regularly for Ironbark Resources, a Web site devoted to promoting Australian culture. In the following viewpoint, he argues that the large U.S. population and economy make it difficult for Australian cultural products to compete with American ones. As a result, Australia is saturated with American television, music, and pop culture. Australians adopt American language, fashion, and cultural attitudes, and many may even have more general knowledge of America than of Australia. Guild concludes that the omnipresence of American culture damages Australia's cultural identity and hurts cultural diversity worldwide.

As you read, consider the following questions:

1. What are some American words and phrases that Guild says have infiltrated Australia?

2. What is the emergency telephone number in Australia, and what do some Australians dial instead, according to Guild?

3. What does the concept of a "battler" mean in Australia, and what American concept does Guild say has replaced it?

Andrew Guild, "The Americanisation of Australian Culture: Discussing the Cultural Influence of the USA upon Our Nation's Way of Life," Ironbark Resources, July 2004. Reproduced by permission of the author.

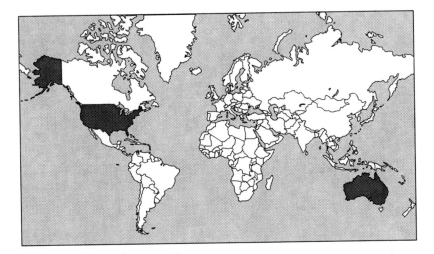

Americanisation is the effect upon a local culture by the long-term and large-scale importation of elements of a crass consumerist culture founded in the USA. It is a commercial culture of Coca-Cola and Pepsi, Hungry Jack's [Australian franchisee of Burger King] and McDonald's. It is a television culture of Jerry Springer and Oprah Winfrey, *The Simpsons* and Mickey Mouse, and "reality shows" (such as *Survivor* and *Big Brother*).

Overwhelmed by America's Size

The Americanisation of Australia's culture is a sad and terrible thing. It is a process whereby ordinary Australians are bombarded every day with images of American lifestyle, so much that it merges almost unnoticed into their own lifestyle. It is a process whereby our homegrown entertainment industry is overwhelmed by the enormous powerhouse of the American economy, with drastic effects upon the modern Australian nation.

As the USA has a population base of over 290 million, along with a successful economy, it has meant that the American population has a large amount of money that is surplus to basic requirements, and that therefore may be devoted to the luxuries of leisure and entertainment, hence the development of such a huge entertainment industry.

Due to economies of scale, it is proportionately cheaper—and more profitable—for the American entertainment industry to produce movies, television shows, etc., than it is for the local entertainment industry to produce the same in Australia. Once American entertainment businesses have made their money on a TV series, any sales of those productions to overseas markets (such as Australia) is pure profit. Therefore, American businesses can afford to sell TV shows to the Australian TV networks for below-cost prices (a practice called "product-dumping"), effectively undercutting the sale of local TV productions—hence, fewer local productions are made, and fewer Australian shows are seen on TV.

Our homegrown entertainment industry is overwhelmed by the enormous powerhouse of the American economy, with drastic effects upon the modern Australian nation.

Facing the economic Goliath of the American entertainment industry, our local industry cannot compete. If it weren't for Australian laws ensuring a certain amount of local content, along with some government funding and tax breaks, Australia's movie and television producers would be in dire straits.

As is the case in much of the developed world, ordinary Australians spend many hours watching TV (especially Australian youth), with the result that we are subtly influenced by its content—whether we want to be or not, whether we are aware of it or not. Due to the massive amount of American content on television, especially during prime time, Australia's culture and way of life is being heavily influenced by American culture and its trends.

Tearlach Hutcheson, an Australian living in the USA, said that

All my life I have been raised predominantly on Hollywood cinema, and Hollywood cinema has never taught me to be an Australian. Instead, it has taught me to be an American. I do not believe that this is a result of living in the US for many years because these were feelings that I had before I came to the US. I believe that even in Australia my fellow Australians experience a fate very similar to mine.

Since 1918 Hollywood cinema has dominated the world, and even earlier, it has dominated the Australian market-place. As a result of this hegemony, Australians, through cinematic exposure, have been raised with a US belief system. However, with the reemergence of the Australian film industry in the seventies [1970s], and the use of cinema by the [Gough] Whitlam government to rid Australia of US and British influences, I believe national identity has slowly begun to be reestablished for Australians.

The American influence upon our society can easily be seen in our language, fashions, general knowledge, and cultural mind-set.

Language and Fashion

American words (or common general English words, now laden with an Americanised meaning or application) and American phrases have buried themselves deep within the Australian language, often without our being aware of their origin.

American words: babe, bro, dude, hoe, homies, ok, whatever

American phrases: chill out; like totally; you go, girl; you're so busted

The computer world also brings American influence. Most major computer applications originate from American companies, such as Microsoft, and therefore, by default, encourage the spread of American English in the spelling of words— when computer programmes are set to recognise American

English rather than British or Australian English, such as in the usage of our/or and sation/zation (for example, favouring "color" over "colour", "organization" over "organisation"). [Whilst typing this article, my copy of Microsoft Word automatically changed my typing of "recognise" to "recognize"—with no prompt or warning—and it was only by luck (or diligence?) that I noticed the change]. With the youth in Western societies heavily reliant upon computers, such "hidden influences" can only add to the cumulative effect of Americanisation.

Professor Pam Peters (associate professor in Linguistics at Macquarie University), noted the results of one linguistics researcher:

> Younger respondents were always more regular users of the American options, and this, by sociolinguistic principle, suggests the way of the future. The longer-term effect is already evident in the considerable number of Americanisms, both popular and professional expressions (from OK to paramedic) which have been absorbed over the last six decades.

As Bruce Moore [author of *Speaking Our Language: The Story of Australian English*] says,

> Contemporary teenspeak comes from the world of teenage popular culture, and this culture is largely American. . . . Listen to a teenager speak, and his or her language will be peppered with Americanisms.

Many people used to slavishly follow Paris fashions (and some still do), however that trend has become more diversified nowadays, and is generally limited to the upper end of the market.

However, the American influence upon streetwear can often be seen; for instance, in the "hip-hop" rapper-style fashions worn by many teenagers; along with a profusion of bandanas and baseball caps (especially when worn back-to-front, in the American style).

Australian Slang

- *Bingle:* motor vehicle accident
- *Bludger:* lazy person
- *Cactus:* dead, not functioning
- *Drink with the flies:* to drink alone
- *Footy:* Australian rules football
- *Gobsmacked:* surprised, astonished
- *Hooroo:* goodbye
- *Jumbuck:* sheep
- *Lollies:* sweets, candies
- *Mystery bag:* a sausage
- *Outback:* interior of Australia
- *Prezzy:* present, gift
- *Swagman:* tramp, hobo
- *Yobbo:* an uncouth person

"Australian Slang,"
April 22, 2010. www.koalanet.com.au.

American influences loom large over the clothing industry, especially the youth market, with brands such as Nike (sport), Wu-Tang (hip-hop), and Levi's jeans.

General Knowledge

Through the saturation of our television networks with American movies, situation comedies, and assorted other TV shows,

Australians often know more about the USA than they do about their own country. A minor survey carried out by this author asked Australian-born subjects to list the states, native tribes, and national leaders of both Australia and the USA; sadly, most people could name more of those from America, rather than from Australia. The results were an indication of the deep American influence upon our society. It would be interesting to see the same survey conducted by a major polling company, although similar results would be expected.

Through the saturation of our television networks with American movies, situation comedies, and assorted other TV shows, Australians often know more about the USA than they do about their own country.

It has even been reported that, after having been inundated with a wide diet of American police/crime shows, some people in Australia have dialed 911 (the emergency telephone number in the USA) instead of 000 (the Australian emergency number).

Also, whether via print or via computers (especially on the Internet), sorting out the American date system from the Australian date system can also bring its own problems—is 7.4.2004 to be read as "7th of April, 2004" (Australian) or as "July 4th, 2004" (American).

The American Cultural Mind-Set

Perhaps most unfortunate of all, many Australians have begun to adopt an American mind-set. This might not be so awful if it was that of small-town America, but instead it is the crass mind-set of the major cities where much of American television and movie entertainment is set and produced: Los Angeles, Washington [D.C.], and New York ("The Big Apple", which has a reputation for thinking money is far more important than people).

For instance, it is only in recent years that we have seen the emergence in Australia of the concept of "loser"; in the past, someone who had fallen on hard times would be termed as a "battler", implicit in which is a struggle to rise up again; whereas it is quite common nowadays to hear such people referred to as "losers", a nasty and disdainful phrase, implicit in which is the idea that such a person is destined to always be at "the bottom of the pile" and to be somewhat beneath contempt.

The "reality shows" genre, originating in the USA, is another example of crass Americanisation that adversely affects our cultural mind-set. All these shows have a common theme of making people look bad, and of individuals being encouraged to stab each other in the back to win. Exactly what kind of culture, morality, and mind-set is this going to foster in our nation's youth? Certainly not a good one. Is crass Americanisation going to bring about a Western culture that is steeped in selfishness, nastiness, and backstabbing? . . .

American influence is creating an urban Western culture that is much the same worldwide.

Like all cultural exchanges, Americanisation does not occur on a one-way street. There are foreign influences upon the USA as well; however, the flow of traffic is definitely in favour of the Americans. It would appear that whilst American influence is flowing outbound to the world on a ten-lane highway, the inbound traffic pedals along on a bicycle path.

American influence is creating an urban Western culture that is much the same worldwide—no matter whether you are in New York, London, Paris, Berlin, Rome, or Sydney. In this globalist world, living in a consumerist climate, saturated by Americanised culture, many people from many different Western nations are now wearing the same style of clothes, eating the same types of junk food, watching the same television shows, and listening to the same music—and this domination by American popular culture comes at the expense of traditional cultures.

The Americanisation of culture, in Australia and across the world, is not a positive development. It is enormously detrimental to our national identity, and is destructive to the cultural diversity of nations worldwide.

Japan Is Replacing America as a Force for Pop Culture Globalization

Amelia Newcomb

Amelia Newcomb is a fellow with the International Reporting Project. In the following viewpoint, she notes that the United States has long dominated international pop culture. Today, however, Japanese cultural products such as manga (comics) and anime (cartoons) are becoming global phenomena and are challenging American dominance. Japanese popular culture is becoming popular throughout the world, including in the United States.

As you read, consider the following questions:

1. What is *The Drops of the Gods*, and where is it popular other than Japan?
2. According to ICv2.com, what was the dollar amount of total manga sales in the United States in 2007?
3. In 2008, artists from what countries sent submissions to the International Manga Award in Japan?

Just two decades ago, Japan's image in the world was of an economic juggernaut, challenging America and other industrialized nations with its push for dominance in everything

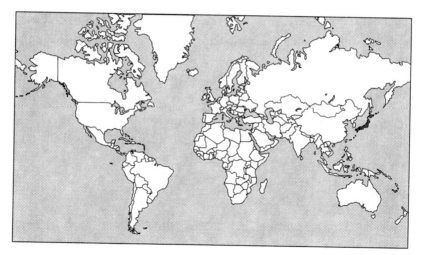

from microchips to supercomputers. Discussion of Japanese culture typically referenced the traditional and offbeat worlds of, say, Kabuki or sumo.

Cool Japan

Today, Japan sets the trends in what's cool. Sarah Palin's famous glasses came from a Japanese designer. Tokyo has the most Michelin-starred restaurants in the world, with eight of them earning three stars. Even America's favorite food show, *Iron Chef*, is a Japanese import. Japanese women are pushing the limits of literary pop culture with blogs and cell phone novels. Japanese comics occupy ever-greater shelf space in bookstores, and anime-influenced movies like *The Dark Knight* and *Spider-Man 3* find huge audiences in the West.

Today, Japan sets the trends in what's cool.

What all these media share is a nuanced Japanese aesthetic that has infiltrated global sensibilities—a sort of new "soft power" for Japan. In the process, they're challenging delineations of good and evil from the world's main purveyor of pop culture, Hollywood, as well as American ideals of the lone action-hero.

"The American 20th-century ideal of the individual super-hero is wearing thin," says Roland Kelts, professor at the University of Tokyo and author of *Japanamerica: How Japanese Pop Culture Has Invaded the U.S.* "The Japanese model is of self-denial and the sublimation of selfish desires for the sake of group harmony. This is becoming a multi-polar world. The desire to be a part of something harmonious rather than the leader of a pack is growing."

The Rise of Manga

Most weekdays, manga [Japanese comics] creators Shin Kibayashi and his sister, Yuko, can be found sitting elbow to elbow in their modest studio in a stylish section of Tokyo. She types dialogue while he comments. She does the same as he sketches. They switch roles—effortlessly—as the spirit moves them.

The world they work in is not one of American-style comic strips. Their serial cartoons—which are regularly bound into large volumes—follow sophisticated characters and plots over long periods of time, much like a soap opera.

The team's work spans the spectrum, from the *Kindaichi Case Files*, a detective series aimed at boys to the soccer manga *Shoot!* to *The Drops of the Gods*, a series for adults that focuses on wine and is read weekly by 500,000 Japanese. In France and Korea, the series is so popular that sales of wine brands mentioned in the comic often spike.

Shin says he's noticed a dramatic rise in interest in their work. "It took a long time, but manga's role has developed citizenship everywhere," he says.

In France last year [2007], for example, 1,787 foreign comic books were translated—64 percent of them Japanese. In the US, total manga sales in 2007 rose about 5 percent, to more than $210 million, according to ICv2.com, a trade Web site. Otakon, a convention devoted to Japanese pop culture in Baltimore, saw a record-breaking 26,000-plus attendees this past summer.

Shin says a plus for manga is the latitude they give the reader. "A significant characteristic is that there's not good and bad only," he says as he and Yuko sit in the entertainment room of his airy European-style home.

Daily life has many areas of gray, the two artists say—and it's incumbent upon them to explore them. That approach applies to young people as well, though they emphasize their sensitivity to young readers' impressionability.

Shin notes that TV, for example, would skirt showing drug use. But in manga, "I will show it, while at the same time making it clear that something must or could be done," he says. "Manga is an experimental medium, so you can explore how to influence boys not to do drugs."

"To readers, the manga's world is more real than Hollywood movies," Yuko adds. "In spite of the fact that the story is fantasy, the way characters [behave] in manga is more realistic."

In France last year [2007] . . . 1,787 foreign comic books were translated—64 percent of them Japanese.

Shin says that 50 years ago, people had much sharper delineations of who was good and who was evil in the world. "Now the world has changed. Nobody is sure who is good or who is evil. . . . The whole world is becoming borderless and unstable. The manga world's ambiguity has become realistic."

Japan's Influence Is Growing

That sense of familiarity and ambiguity is key. "There's nothing casual about this form," says Gonzalo Ferreyra, a vice president at VIZ Media, the largest US importer of manga and anime. In the past five years, he says, the company has seen high double-digit increases in sales. "These are stories that . . . can sustain interest for several dozen volumes."

BookScan Top 20 Graphic Novels in January 2010

The chart shows the top selling graphic novels sold through bookstores in the U.S. Out of 20, 14 are Japanese. Two others (#10 and 13) are in a Japanese manga style.

Rank	Title	Author	Publisher
1	Yu-Gi-Oh! Gx Vol. 4	Naoyuki Kageyama	Viz Media
2	The Book of Genesis Illus. by R. Crumb HC	Robert Crumb	W. W. Norton
3	Naruto Vol. 47	Masashi Kishimoto	Viz Media
4	Fullmetal Alchemist Vol. 22	Arakawa Hiromu	Viz Media
5	Watchmen TP	Alan Moore	DC Comics
6	The Zombie Survival Guide: Recorded Attacks	Max Brooks	Three Rivers
7	Black Butler Vol. 1	Yana Toboso	Yen Press
8	One Piece Vol. 24	Eiichiro Oda	Viz Media
9	Naruto Vol. 46	Masashi Kishimoto	Viz Media
10	Maximum Ride: The Manga Vol. 2	James Patterson	Yen Press
11	Vampire Knight Vol. 8	Matsuri Hino	Viz Media
12	One Piece Vol. 25	Eiichiro Oda	Viz Media
13	Maximum Ride: The Manga Vol. 1	James Patterson	Yen Press
14	One Piece Vol. 26	Eiichiro Oda	Viz Media
15	One Piece Vol. 27	Eiichiro Oda	Viz Media
16	One Piece Vol. 28	Eiichiro Oda	Viz Media
17	Vampire Knight Vol. 1	Matsuri Hino	Viz Media
18	The Walking Dead Vol. 11: Fear the Hunters	Robert Kirkman	Image Comics
19	Bleach Vol. 29	Tite Kubo	Tokyopop
20	Death Note Vol. 1	Tsugumi Ohba	Viz Media

TAKEN FROM: "Yu-Gi-Oh! Dominates GN Chart in January," *icv2.com*, February 8, 2010. www.icv2.com.

Indeed, many readers commit to manga over decades. Suzue Miuchi, who is relaunching one of Japan's longest-running girls' manga, *Glass Mask*, points to letters from fans who say they have overcome weakness by tracking the life of Maya, an actress whose strong will to live helps her overcome seemingly insurmountable obstacles.

"I have always felt that I give readers many things," says Ms. Miuchi, whose gentle demeanor belies an intense schedule of sleeping part of the day and working through the night on the series, which has run for more than 30 years. "But I am not asking them to take a certain message. You can take away what you want."

That's part of the appeal. "It's nice to be reminded that there's no one way of looking at, or surviving in, or laughing at, the world, but we all must, in the end, manage these things," Mr. Ferreyra says.

In true Japanese style, the point is made without fanfare. "I always feel like US culture bashes down doors, while Japanese culture seeps in under the door," says Bruce Rutledge, publisher of Chin Music Press in Seattle.

I always feel like US culture bashes down doors, while Japanese culture seeps in under the door.

He points to cartoons that kids watch, but don't specifically associate with Japan. Or take sushi: "It went from being 'Gross! Raw fish!' to the food of beautiful people," he says. Japanese culture became all the rage, he adds, because "it was exotic, but it made sense or it entertained us, or both."

That point is not lost on the Japanese government, which sees the "soft power" possibilities of the country's artistic prowess. Its consular Web sites tout manga and anime. Government brochures share information via manga-style booklets. And Prime Minister Taro Aso is perhaps the first leader of a major nation to trumpet his credentials as a comic book geek, though to limited success.

This year [2008], Japan awarded its second International Manga Award to a Hong Kong artist—who beat out submissions from 46 countries, including Indonesia, Russia, Brazil, Britain, Saudi Arabia, and Spain.

"To improve your image in the world, you have to make use of all the tools available," says Kenjiro Monji, Japan's former ambassador to Iraq who recently became director general of public diplomacy, a post that was established three years ago. He is quick to note that pop culture doesn't need government's promotional hand. But, he says, he can play a role as Japan takes note of a three-fold increase since 1990—to 3 million—in those studying Japanese. The number of Americans studying in Japan rose 13 percent between 2005 and 2007, according to the New York-based Institute of International Education. "We can use the attractive power of popular culture as an introduction," says Mr. Monji.

Global Pop Culture Must Adapt to Local Conditions

Carl Wilson

Carl Wilson is a writer and editor at the Globe and Mail *and runs the music blog Zoilus.com. In the following viewpoint, he notes that Canadian pop star Céline Dion is popular worldwide. However, he argues that she attained that popularity by adapting her songs and style to different local cultures. The result, he concludes, is not homogenization but hybridization, with each part of the world adapting the singer to fit its own culture and needs.*

As you read, consider the following questions:

1. What are some of the soundtracks on which Céline Dion has sung?
2. Why did Sony have to release a number of different versions of Céline Dion's greatest hits album in 1999?
3. In what neighborhoods in Jamaica was Céline Dion's music particularly popular, according to Garnette Cadogan?

Unlike most musicians, who establish themselves on a local scene and then aim for wider renown, Céline took the planet for her stage from the beginning. Her 1982 win at

Carl Wilson, *Let's Talk About Love: A Journey to the End of Taste*, Lynn, MA: Continuum, 2007, pp. 43–50. Copyright © 2007 by Carl Wilson. All rights reserved. Republished with permission of The Continuum International Publishing Group, Inc., conveyed through Copyright Clearance Center, Inc.

the now-defunct Tokyo song contest was succeeded by her bigger victory in 1988 representing Switzerland at the Eurovision Song Contest, the five-decade-old Cheeseball Olympics of pop music, the most-watched ongoing musical event on Earth, with an annual audience estimated at 300 million. Eurovision traffics almost exclusively in major-key, upbeat tunes, limited to three minutes and burdened with somehow simultaneously representing the competing nations' souls and eschewing any hint of chauvinism. Though it began with performers wearing local costume and singing in their native tongues, an "international language" requirement was added in later years by the TV networks that administer it, to make it more commercially viable, so English and French songs predominate. If you've ever seen Italian variety TV, with its blowsy hostesses and pompadoured hosts, you have the general aesthetic. As British Eurovision fan Mike Atkinson wrote in 1996 for Slate.com, "[There] is nothing remotely hip about Eurovision, which generally runs at least 10 years behind developments in youth-based genres, if not 20." Costumes are "florid" and dance routines "frantic," and the prevailing genres are power ballads, bubblegum pop, anthems of international tolerance and what Atkinson calls "'ethereal folksy-ethnic,' which makes much use of Riverdance-style choreography, gypsy fiddles, panpipes and the like." However, as he notes, "this stylistic conservatism does ensure a continuing appeal to the sort of traditional, multigenerational, family-based demographic that is rapidly disappearing in our tightly, segmented, multichannel age." Eurovision was made for Céline and she for it. She was the bookies' favorite from the start.

But her world-beating doesn't stop at her status as arguably the world's most successful talent show act. She emulated the likes of Whitney Houston by making sure that she had a Hollywood tie-in with each of her 90s English albums: in 1992 it was the title song, with Peabo Bryson, on *Beauty and the Beast*; to boost 1993's *The Colour of My Love* she sang

"When I Fall in Love" on the soundtrack of *Sleepless in Seattle*; for *Falling into You*, it was *Up Close and Personal*; and of course *Titanic* for *Let's Talk About Love* (though only by a whisker: James Cameron had to be talked into having a theme song, and Céline initially hated "My Heart Will Go On"). Such projects not only enable her to piggyback on the movie-distribution system, they can get her a global audience at the Oscars. Singing at the 1996 Atlanta Olympics had a similar effect.

Unlike most musicians, who establish themselves on a local scene and then aim for wider renown, Céline took the planet for her stage from the beginning.

However, as the University of Leicester's Masahiro Yasuda points out in his 1999 paper "Localising Dion," Team Céline has gone far beyond those standard means of overseas seduction: They have coordinated with Sony A&R people around the world to tailor singles, bonus tracks and collaborations to each major market. According to a Japanese Sony rep Yasuda interviewed, A. Miyai, early in Céline's career the company decided "no Hollywoodish artist would be possible anymore, apart from the existing ones, such as Michael Jackson"; global markets now demanded another approach. Sony put out a call for ideas to all its offices. In France, it led to Céline's work with Jean-Jacques Goldman. In Japan, where domestic music dominated seventy percent of the market, "The almost unprecedented promotion strategy . . . was to promote Céline Dion through a network of the Japanese mainstream genre *kayokyoku*, which generally relies on an 'image-song' strategy of tie-ins with TV ads and soap operas." A *kayokyoku* song is also rushed to karaoke, "which almost systematically excludes international catalogues whose peripheral rights are more complicated to exploit." In 1995 Céline and producer David Foster met the producers of a romantic soap on Fuji TV to create a theme song and "To Love You More," backed by local Sony act Kryzler and Kompany, became the first No. 1 single by a foreigner in Japan in twelve years.

She didn't originate this Esperanto-pop capitalism . . . but Céline is its modern model citizen.

Many other artists would mimic the strategy, but it is only the most dramatic example of Céline being customized to local audiences. When Latin America was a weak point, she began recording songs in Spanish, including *"Amar Haciendo el Amor,"* included on some editions of *Let's Talk About Love*. Ad campaigns, tours, TV specials and singles are carefully matched with cultural demands. In 1999, when a Céline greatest hits album was in the works, Sony realized it would have to release several versions to reflect the various Célines belonging to audiences around the world.

She didn't originate this Esperanto-pop capitalism. For that, look to someone like Greece's Nana Mouskouri, whose 60s-to-80s albums were mini-Berlitz courses. But Céline is its modern model citizen, in part because she's not American. Other Canadian songbirds have been particularly keen students, with Shania Twain adding a Bollywoodish "worldbeat" bonus disc to 2002's *Up!* for international markets or Avril Lavigne releasing 2007 hit single "Girlfriend" in eight languages, including Mandarin, and starring in a Japanese manga comic. Note that Avril is also on Sony, which is, after all, an Asian concern. The assumption that multinational corporations propagate a Western point of view overlooks that increasingly they are not Western based. The Japanese Sony A&R rep told Yasuda that his job was to be "right in front of overseas artists in recording studios, so as to inform them about their Japanese fans and what is expected of them."

Céline has chafed now and then—in 1996, she told *Time*, "I didn't want to do the Spanish song. What do they want me to do next? Learn Japanese?" But two years later, she did sing in Japanese, for another Fuji TV soap opera. In 1999, after performing on the runway of Hong Kong's decommissioned Kai Tak Airport, she was asked at a press conference if she'd be interested in learning Chinese, and answered, "That'd be great! I'd love to learn every language in the world. When you're an artist, a musician, you have a musical ear. It's easier for you to learn languages."

Now a successful artist has to figuratively become *local by fulfilling entertainment conventions in other parts of the world. It is less homogenization than hybridization of cultures.*

This is becoming the norm, and as Yasuda argues, it's not like the Coca-Colonization stereotype. Now a successful artist has to figuratively *become* local by fulfilling entertainment conventions in other parts of the world. It is less homogenization than hybridization of cultures. As Jan Nederveen Pieterse of the Institute of Social Studies in the Hague writes, "How do we come to terms with phenomena such as Thai boxing by Moroccan girls in Amsterdam, Asian rap in London, Irish bagels, Chinese tacos and Mardi Gras Indians in the United States . . . ? Cultural experiences, past or present, have not been simply moving in the direction of cultural uniformity and standardisation." He suggests what we're witnessing is a "creolisation of global culture." It does not follow that creolization will take a standard form. Localism is ignored, as Céline's marketers know, at peril. Likewise the global-hegemony model presumes there won't be reciprocal cultural influence on the West, but the counterevidence is all around us: Asian video-game music, for example, is arguably among the most pervasive influences on young pop musicians now. And as Pieterse points out, with the exception of isolated indigenous groups, civilization and hybridization have been synonymous for centuries.

This is not an answer to exploitation and inequality. But the presumption that the world will automatically become *more like us* is itself chauvinism. Contrary to globalization cheerleader Thomas Friedman's best-selling sloganeering, the world is not going "flat," never has and never will, unless you look through a two-dimensional screen. Yet some Western critics of hegemony present merely a negative image of American triumphalism. In George W. Bush's case, it is wishful thinking; in theirs, apocalyptic thinking; but both operate as if the totalization of their own culture were an inevitability, despite all signals of how improbable that is.

The presumption that the world will automatically become more like us *is itself chauvinism.*

Some of that self-absorption can be heard in the wide-eyed horror with which Western witnesses relate Céline's popularity abroad. Local accounts are subtler, indicating how commercial music is redeployed in everyday life for people's own purposes. One of the most astounding tales of Céline's global flexibility comes to me from Jamaican-American music critic Garnette Cadogan, who says she may be Jamaica's most popular non-native musical figure. And not just for grandmas.

"I wish I could give you an explanation beyond Jamaicans' love for saccharine tunes, but that may be satisfactory enough," Cadogan wrote me.

And the places she turns up in Jamaica are all the more curious. I remember being at strand-system dances and hearing everyone from Bob Marley to Kenny Rogers (yes, Kenny Rogers) to Sade to Yellowman to Beenie Man being blasted at top volume while the crowd danced and drank up a storm. But once the selector (DJ in American parlance) began to play a Céline Dion song, the crowd went buck wild and some people started firing shots in the air.... I also remember always hearing Céline Dion blasting at high volume whenever I passed through volatile and dangerous neighborhoods, so much that it became a cue to me to walk, run or drive faster if I was ever in a neighborhood I didn't know and heard Céline Dion mawking over the airwaves.

I sometimes shared this little anecdote with other Jamaican friends, only for them to laughingly comment that they had a similar practice. The unofficial rule seemed to be, "If you hear Céline Dion then you're in the wrong place." That's not to say that roughnecks (as gangsters are also called in Jamaica) are the only ones who appreciate and publicly show their love for Saccharine Céline. It's just that, for some reason, they show her more love than just about any other group.

Cadogan asked around, including a few roughnecks, and the reason given was, "to quote one fellow, 'Bad man have fi play love tune fi show 'dat them a lova too.'"

The Pentagon apparently has the same idea. In the run-up to the Iraq war, the US was reported to be wooing Iraqis with a radio station broadcasting Céline to show the West's softer side, alongside Arabic-singing stars, all programmed by Iraqi-American staff in Washington. (Propagandists apparently listen to local informants in a way the occupation forces haven't mastered.) Indeed, comparisons between Céline and Middle Eastern divas surfaced over and over in my research. She may even recognize them herself: An article on the comeback of Iranian superstar Googoosh mentioned Céline attended Googoosh's concert in Toronto.

Yet when reports came out that part of US military intelligence's "no-touch torture" techniques, used to circumvent the Geneva Conventions, include blasting loops of loud music at prisoners night and day—a practice that should sicken any music lover—I came across scads of sniggering downpage editorials and blog posts quipping that "they ought to use Céline Dion": surely *that* would break any recalcitrant P.O.W. In reality, it would be turning some of their favorite music against them. After artist Paul Chan went to Baghdad in 2003 with American activist group Iraq Peace Team, he told the *Omaha World-Herald* that there, "Everyone loves Céline Dion. For some reason they see her as the pinnacle of sadness. Her songs speak to the plight of the Iraqi people." He added, "It makes me giggle to think that. It makes them more human. And the more human they seem, the harder it is to kill them." It's a patronizing remark, but better than the torture jokes' implication that affection for Céline might as well be a *reason* to kill them.

"Everyone loves Céline Dion. For some reason they [Iraqis] see her as the pinnacle of sadness. Her songs speak to the plight of the Iraqi people."

What's remarkable in many of the stories about Céline's international presence is how moving they are. Think of Chinese gymnast Sang Lan, who was paralyzed in a fall at the 1998 Goodwill Games, and had Céline come to her hospital room in New York and give a private, *a capella* performance. *People* magazine reported: "Says the determined 17-year-old through an interpreter, 'When she goes to Hong Kong next year, I'll find a way to walk there, if that's what it takes.'"

Then there was the Iranian-Canadian activist, Neda Hassani, twenty-six, who immolated herself outside the French embassy in London in June 2003, trying to force the release from French prisons of several leaders of the leftist People's Mujahedin of Iran, which opposes the Iranian clerical regime. (After her death, some were set free.) The *Ottawa Citizen*'s report of her burial at Pinecrest Cemetery in Ottawa ended, "Amid a glorious pile of wilting flowers laid days before at Ms. Hassani's funeral, a child sang Céline Dion's 'My Heart Will Go On' through a makeshift public-address system, and the tears flowed."

Finally, when I think of how Céline's global impact complicates my sense of her and of the world, I think of another twenty-six-year-old, Mohammed Ahmad Younis, a Baghdad barber. In 2005, he appeared on *Iraq Star*, the Iraqi version of *American Idol*, in which the prize was a record deal—and a ticket out of Iraq. The show was seen as sacrilegious by local militants; contestants were beaten and ostracized. Younis's own girlfriend dumped him for going "too far outside the mainstream." But he still competed, under the pseudonym "Saif from Babylon," because, as he told the *Los Angeles Times*, "I'd rather die and be dead than stay alive and be dead." Wearing sunglasses, a "punk" haircut, fake-leather jeans, platform shoes, blue contact lenses and a black *Star Trek* T-shirt, he performed a tune by Lebanese diva Fairuz, and then encored with "My Heart Will Go On." Promoting him to the next round, one of the judges said, "Good job—I felt as if I was on the *Titanic*."

Younis must have felt that way, too. Sometimes it seems we're all on that damn boat together.

Periodical Bibliography

The following articles have been selected to supplement the diverse views presented in this chapter.

Tyler Cowen	"For Some Countries, America's Popular Culture Is Resistible," *New York Times*, February 22, 2007. www.nytimes.com.
Brian Knowlton	"Globalization, According to the World, Is a Good Thing. Sort Of," *New York Times*, October 5, 2007. www.nytimes.com.
Marwan M. Kraidy	"American Pop Culture: A Commodity or an Ideology?" *Global Media Journal*, Fall 2008.
Amy Lai	"Ignorning Hello Kitty: Globalization and Resistance in Austria," Suite101.com, August 14, 2007. http://popculture.suite101.com.
Rama Lakshmi	"Call Centers Are Fodder for India's Pop Culture: Bollywood Movie Is Latest Manifestation," *Washington Post*, October 20, 2008. www.washingtonpost.com.
Andrew Leonard	"Don't You Wish Your Girlfriend Was a Slumdog Like Me?" Salon.com, March 24, 2009. www.salon.com.
Vera Mackie	"Transnational Bricolage: Gothic Lolita and the Political Economy of Fashion," *Intersections: Gender and Sexuality in Asia and the Pacific*, no. 20, April 2009. http://intersections.anu.edu.au.
Richard Morgan	"What Turks Are Watching: A New Wave of Anti-American Pop Culture," *Slate*, June 13, 2006. www.slate.com.
Bill Randall	"Bring the Noise," *Comics Journal*, December 30, 2009. www.tcj.com.
Sam Wardle	"The Bollywood Invasion," GlobalEnvision.org, October 10, 2005. www.globalenvision.org.

CHAPTER 2

Popular Culture and Intellectual Property Rights

In New Zealand, a New Download Law Is Unfair and Unworkable

Internet Service Providers Association of New Zealand

Internet Service Providers Association of New Zealand (ISPANZ) is a nonprofit industry group that represents most Internet service providers operating in New Zealand. In the following viewpoint, ISPANZ says that a New Zealand anti-downloading law will force Internet service providers to disconnect customers if they are accused of illegal downloading. The organization says that this law is unfair and unworkable. In addition, ISPANZ argues that the law will hurt commerce and economic development.

As you read, consider the following questions:

1. What kinds of organizations does Jamie Baddeley fear may have their Internet service wrongfully disconnected as a result of accusations against employees?

2. According to Baddeley, who is likely to sue ISPs if they disconnect service, and who is likely to sue them if they do not?

3. What kind of ISPs does Baddeley believe will be targeted by copyright holders?

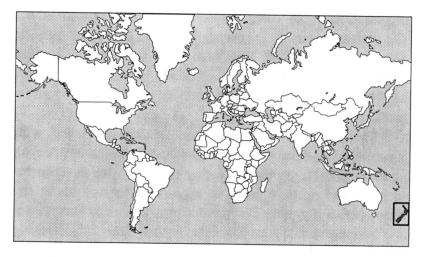

The Internet Service Providers Association [of New Zealand] (ISPANZ) respectfully requests that the government not bring into force Section 92A of the Copyright [Amendment] Act on February 28 [2009]. Section 92A is a poorly constructed law designed to force ISPs [Internet service providers] to cut off the Internet access of those accused of repeat infringement of copyright.

ISPANZ notes that the select committee considering the original bill, which was chaired by Hon Gerry Brownlee, [of the National Party] rejected this approach, but the previous government [led by the Labour Party] reinserted the clauses in a last minute action, [before the 2008 election, in which the National Party defeated the Labour Party] making New Zealand a guinea pig for experimental cyberlaw.

The Law Can Still Be Changed

ISPANZ President Jamie Baddeley says the select committee got it right and the new government still has a chance to take corrective action.

"If Section 92A is allowed to come in, ISPs will have to disconnect organisations such as businesses, public libraries, government agencies, etc., as a result of accusations that an employee has used their computers for illegal downloading. The customer may be innocent, there may be an error, or the downloading may well have been done by a virus. Everyday Kiwis [a nickname for New Zealanders] with a computer that has been inadvertently hacked may have their Internet access terminated.

"This law needs to go back to the drawing board, with government re-examining the issue and finding a better path forward. ISPANZ would be happy to work with government agencies and rights holders to explore better options in the same open and progressive manner in which it has approached the Telecommunications Carriers' Forum Copyright working party," says Baddeley.

"Under section 92A we'll be damned if we do and damned if we don't."

ISPANZ notes with concern rights holders' claim that 60–80 percent of all Internet traffic is peer-to-peer sharing of copyright infringing files. What needs to be recognised here is that unless rights holders can 100 percent guarantee that accusation equals guilt then businesses (who produce little or no peer-to-peer traffic) are at risk of being taken down through a wrongful accusation. ISPANZ believes the rights holders need to qualify their claims about businesses and their use of the Internet.

Baddeley says ISPs are being placed in a terrible position.

"Under Section 92A we'll be damned if we do and damned if we don't. We'll be faced with dealing with an accusation, not proven, of a copyright infringement and making a very difficult judgment call. If we decide in favour of our customers, we risk being sued by global media powerhouses. If we decide in favour of the rights holder and disconnect a customer from the Internet, we risk being sued by customers for breach of contract. Disconnecting customers goes against everything we do."

Baddeley notes support on this issue from every major ICT [information and communications technology] group in the country, including the Telecommunication Carriers' Forum, the NZ [New Zealand] Computer Society, the Telecommunications Users Association of New Zealand, InternetNZ, and others. Other groups, including a group of artists, have also come out against Section 92A.

The Law Is Anti-Development

Baddeley says draconian laws to disconnect Internet access also go against what New Zealand has been doing in respect to broadband, social connectivity, and economic development.

Draconian laws to disconnect Internet access . . . go against what New Zealand has been doing in respect to broadband, social connectivity, and economic development.

"Over the last decade or more we've seen excellent progress in connecting the average person with their friends, families and business associates around the world in a way that is better than before. And businesses have had major increases in productivity by having more accessible ICT tools."

A lot of the progress made towards a level, more competitive playing field in the telecommunications market is also in danger of being undermined.

"The worrying thing, as we've seen in Australia, is that it's not the ISPs that carry the bulk of the market that are targeted by copyright holders. It is smaller, more innovative ISPs, who are ill equipped to deal with a major legal battle. It is those innovators that ISPANZ largely comprises of—ISPs who make real progress for their customers. If the smaller ISPs go out of business due to Section 92A, that undoes progress made from a policy perspective."

Top 25 Country Losses to Piracy of Intellectual Property

Country	2008 Losses in Millions of $US
United States	$9,143
China	$6,677
Russia	$4,215
India	$2,768
France	$2,760
United Kingdom	$2,181
Germany	$2,152
Italy	$1,895
Brazil	$1,645
Japan	$1,495
Canada	$1,222
Spain	$1,029
Mexico	$823
Poland	$648
South Korea	$622
Australia	$613
Thailand	$609
Netherlands	$563
Indonesia	$544
Ukraine	$534
Venezuela	$484
Turkey	$468
Sweden	$372
Malaysia	$368
Switzerland	$345

BSA-IDC,
"Sixth Annual BSA-IDC Global Software Piracy Study,"
May 2009. http://global.bsa.org.

ISPANZ recognises the benefits of copyright. Many of its members' customers rely on copyright for their livelihoods. However, ISPANZ has serious concerns whether Section 92A can play a part in protecting it.

"On the one hand we're being asked to enable an economy through global networking and ICT efficiency, and on the other hand we're being asked to stop that connectivity by accusation alone, in order to try to solve another industry's problem with how they make money off their copyright franchises."

In New Zealand, the New Download Law Will Benefit Consumers and Musicians

Campbell Smith

Campbell Smith is chief executive of the Recording Industry Association of New Zealand. In the following viewpoint, he explains that New Zealand is considering a new law that would allow copyright holders to identify those who download large amounts of copyrighted material. Copyright holders could then ask Internet service providers (ISPs) to shut down the accounts of those doing the illegal downloading, disconnecting them from the Internet. Smith says that this is less harsh than prosecuting or suing those who download copyrighted materials. He maintains that the law will help artists protect their copyrights, which will ultimately benefit consumers.

As you read, consider the following questions:

1. According to Smith, by how much has the trade value of recorded music fallen in the ten years before this viewpoint was written?
2. What does Smith say the law will *not* do?
3. Smith says that record companies do not want anyone to lose their Internet accounts, but instead want users to do what?

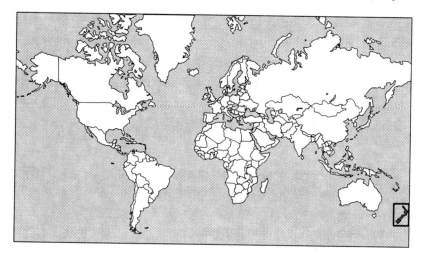

Lawmakers worldwide are getting to grips with how to protect creative content online. All agree with [New Zealand] Prime Minister John Key's assertion that the Internet should not be a "Wild West" where creators' rights are trampled underfoot. Most are working on their own solutions to the problem.

Protection for Rights Holders

New Zealand was at the forefront of tackling the issue with a law that had received bipartisan backing.

Music makers welcomed New Zealand's policy makers tackling this problem, realising that doing nothing was no longer an option. The trade value of recorded music worldwide has fallen by more than a fifth in the past 10 years [that is, before 2009], despite more people than ever using and enjoying it.

The recording industry has transformed its business models, making music available online and on mobile through a variety of different partners. Yet the widespread availability of unlicensed music on the Internet acts as a disincentive to those considering setting up legal services.

The recorded music industry has been working hard to find proportionate and reasonable solutions to tackling online copyright infringement. In some countries, labels have taken legal action against users who have uploaded infringing music to the Internet without permission for millions to download without payment. We believe Section 92A [the New Zealand law] is a better solution for everyone.

The recorded music industry has been working hard to find proportionate and reasonable solutions to tackling online copyright infringement.

In New Zealand, we have looked long and hard at coming up with an effective way of tackling the problem. Internet service providers are in a unique position to help us protect creative content online. It makes sense for the government to facilitate negotiations to ensure that ISPs [Internet service providers] that take action are not undercut by those that do not. Consumers also need to be reassured that what is being done is efficient and proportionate.

In the past few weeks there have been a lot of misleading reports and sensational propaganda about Section 92A. It is not surprising that many have spoken out against the legislation. I would vote against it myself if it was half as bad as it is being portrayed by some of its critics.

Some people have suggested the new law would mean people keeping tabs on what Internet sites people visit or monitoring people's e-mail. That is not true.

Others suggest that under the draft code of conduct designed to implement the law people will be summarily thrown off the Internet for downloading a couple of unlicensed files. That is also not true.

What would happen is simple. Rights holders could log on to public file sharing sites, just as anyone can, and note which

IP [Internet protocol] addresses are being used to upload pre-release music or films or large amounts of copyright-infringing material.

They would then prepare evidence, complete with details of the names of the copyrighted files being uploaded, exact timestamps and the protocol used, and send it to the relevant ISP. They would never see the personal details of the person behind that IP address.

The ISP would then contact its user and warn [him or her] that [he or she was] breaking the law, advise [him or her] not to do it again and provide details of where to enjoy music legally online.

If the user kept breaking the law the ISP could close the Internet account.

I agree with the proposition that users should be able to flag to an independent adjudicator anything they regard as mistaken evidence. This is no sledgehammer. On the contrary, it is a reasonable and much preferable alternative to the lawsuits we've seen in other countries.

This is no sledgehammer. On the contrary, it is a reasonable and much preferable alternative to the lawsuits we've seen in other countries.

There are no human rights issues involved. Preventing copyright infringement is something that ISPs already set out in their terms and conditions.

Record companies and recording artists don't want anyone to lose their Internet accounts. They want users to migrate from using unlicensed services to enjoying music legally online. If this happens, there is then a greater incentive for new players to come in to compete in the legal market.

Section 92A will be great news for consumers who will be able to enjoy a wide choice of artists to listen to.

China Would Benefit from Stronger Intellectual Property Laws

Joe McDonald

Joe McDonald is a business writer for the Associated Press. In the following viewpoint, he reports that rampant piracy in China makes it difficult for China's own industries to benefit from their innovations and cultural products. This is especially the case with computer software, where pirated versions are crippling China's software industry. He suggests that strengthening antipiracy laws and enforcement would benefit Western nations whose goods are being copied, but it would ultimately benefit China even more.

As you read, consider the following questions:

1. How widespread is the use of Kingsoft's Chinese-English dictionary software, and how widespread is the piracy of it?
2. According to U.S. officials, how much do pirated goods exported from China cost legitimate producers every year?
3. Why are Chinese leaders particularly interested in seeing the software industry flourish, according to McDonald?

Joe McDonald, "Piracy Hurting China's Own Industries," *The Washington Post*, July 1, 2006. Copyright © 2006 The Associated Press. Reprinted with permission of the Associated Press.

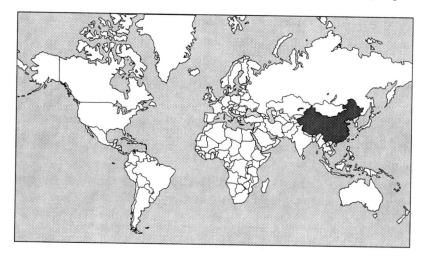

Kingsoft Corp.'s Chinese-English dictionary program is used on most of China's 60 million PCs [personal computers]. That's the good news. The bad news: Kingsoft doesn't make any money from it, because 90 percent of those copies are pirated.

Piracy Makes It Hard to Compete

One by one, the Beijing-based software maker has seen its sales of such popular products destroyed after black market producers flooded the market with cheap copies.

Today, Kingsoft's 600 programmers focus on making what it hopes can't be copied—online games and business and antivirus programs that have to be linked to its own computers in order to function.

"Piracy has had a big impact on us, making it so we can't get powerful and compete with [U.S. software giant] Microsoft," said Ren Jian, a former Microsoft manager who is Kingsoft's chief operating officer [COO].

Kingsoft is far from alone. Rampant Chinese piracy of music, movies and software that raises howls of protest from the United States, Europe and elsewhere is hitting China's fledgling creative industries hardest of all. Robbed of sales in their key home market, companies are short of money to develop new products to compete with foreign rivals.

Losses to piracy are especially damaging at a time when Communist leaders want China to transform itself from the world's low-cost factory into an "innovation society" that makes its own profitable technology and brand names.

China has long been the world's leading source of illegally copied music, movies, designer clothes and other goods. U.S. officials say its exports cost legitimate producers worldwide up to $50 billion a year in lost potential sales.

Rampant Chinese piracy of music, movies and software that raises howls of protest from the United States, Europe and elsewhere is hitting China's fledgling creative industries hardest of all.

At home, sidewalk vendors sell unlicensed DVDs of Chinese movies for as little as 50 cents. Software makers say more than 80 percent of programs used on China's PCs are pirated.

Few brands are immune. A government list released this month [July 2006] of recent major piracy cases included a gang that sold $300,000 worth of fake Wuliangye, a popular Chinese liquor. Another trafficked in counterfeit upmarket Chunghwa cigarettes.

Sporting goods maker Li Ning Co., which has ambitions to expand abroad, says it sees copies of its shoes and athletic clothes in markets alongside Nike and Adidas counterfeits.

Kingsoft, the software maker, aspired to be the "Microsoft of China," but was forced by piracy to stop selling games, a media player and other mass-market programs. Ren, the COO, says the consumer logic is simple: A pirated copy of Kingsoft's Chinese-English dictionary costs one-tenth the $12 price of the real thing.

The onslaught has forced Kingsoft to narrow its product range, with two-thirds of its programmers now working on online role-playing games that players access on Kingsoft's computers for a monthly fee—part of a thriving Chinese market for online games.

Stronger Enforcement Is Needed

President Hu Jintao called attention to piracy's cost to China in a May 27 speech to Communist Party officials. Enforcement "is an urgent need for . . . enhancing the country's core competitiveness," Hu said.

"We should strengthen our law enforcement and lawfully and severely crack down on and effectively curb law-breaking and criminal acts of violating intellectual property rights," he said.

The government has tried to undercut the black market for software by ordering computer makers this year to sell PCs only with legitimate operating systems already installed. Officials have been told to remove pirated software from government computers. Commerce Minister Bo Xilai said in March [2006] that process was under way, but he set no deadline for compliance.

And Chinese companies are fighting back in court. The government says they are responsible for 90 percent of lawsuits filed against Chinese copyright and trademark violators.

Yet trade groups and foreign governments say that despite repeated crackdowns, China's output of pirated goods is rising steadily, along with its rapid economic growth.

Trade groups and foreign governments say that despite repeated crackdowns, China's output of pirated goods is rising steadily, along with its rapid economic growth.

A report in May by the American Chamber of Commerce in China said that 43 percent of 76 U.S. companies surveyed said they have seen an increase in the amount of counterfeiting of their products, while 55 percent said the amount has stayed the same. Only 7 percent saw a decrease.

Losses to piracy have made film studios and music companies reluctant to finance new releases at a time when they might be cashing in on rising foreign interest in Chinese pop culture.

Chinese musicians say piracy makes producing new CDs so unprofitable that they are treated as just promotional material for concerts, which provide performers' real income.

Web sites that carry unlicensed copies of CDs often give away the music for free and make money from advertising. That takes advantage of a provision in Chinese law—one that trade groups are lobbying Beijing to change—that requires pirated goods to be sold before violators can be prosecuted.

Chengdu Xiangsha Music Co., in the southwestern city of Chengdu, got out of its main business of distributing CDs and promoting new performers in 2003 when it saw that losses to piracy "would be huge," said general manager Liu Jiming.

Now Xiangsha focuses on supplying music to Web sites and mobile phone companies, Liu said.

"Things are much better now," he said. "But we are still bothered by illegal downloads and online linking."

Software Piracy Is Especially Damaging

Losses to software piracy are especially damaging to China's plans.

Beijing wants to see the industry flourish, both to create jobs and to reduce reliance on foreign software, which Communist leaders consider a strategic weakness. China has scores of small software companies and its universities produce thousands of programmers every year.

But battered by piracy, software developers are switching from selling products under their own brand names to working as subcontractors for U.S., Indian and other foreign companies—just the anonymous status that Chinese leaders don't want. Most Chinese software companies—such as DHC [Software Co. Ltd.], SinoCom Software Group Ltd., BroadenGate Systems Inc. and UFSoft [Software] Co.—focus on subcontracting for foreign clients instead of selling to the general public.

A report this month by the Business Software Alliance [BSA], a U.S.-based industry group, said 86 percent of software used in China last year [2005] was pirated—one of the world's highest rates—though it said that was an improvement over 2004's figure of 90 percent.

Even though China is the world's No. 2 PC market, "the legal market for software is relatively small, because of the large piracy rate," said Jeffrey Hardee, the BSA's vice president for Asia.

"When the piracy rate is as high as it is, it's hard for (Chinese) producers to develop a market, while the foreign developers have the whole world market," he said.

In a separate report in December, BSA argued that China could see its information technology industries triple in size and create 1.8 million new jobs if its piracy rate were cut by just 10 percentage points over the next four years.

"China could potentially gain more than any other country," the report said.

Ren says the problem is not lack of official enforcement but Chinese consumers, whom he complains don't see that they are supporting innovation when they pay for legitimate goods.

"Ordinary Chinese people don't see anything wrong with buying pirated goods," he said. "We need to change people's attitudes. That is going to take time."

China and India Would Not Benefit from Stronger Intellectual Property Laws

Kevin Donovan

Kevin Donovan has worked at the World Bank's infoDev and serves on the board of Students for Free Culture, an organization that advocates for the public interest in intellectual property. In the following viewpoint, he argues that strong intellectual property rights in China and India tend to give jobs, money, and power to foreign rights holders. Moreover, he says, stronger intellectual property rights have not been shown to encourage innovation. He argues that China and India should keep intellectual property laws weak and should instead encourage innovation through other means, such as open source initiatives and government grants.

As you read, consider the following questions:

1. According to Donovan, what does stronger global intellectual property encourage, which is to America's benefit, but which China and India should not necessarily favor?

2. How much of global R&D (research and development) is carried out in the developed world, according to Donovan?

Kevin Donovan, "Why Increased IP in China and India Is Likely to Disproportionately Benefit the Developed World" and "In China and India, Stronger Intellectual Property Is Unnecessary," Techdirt, July 16 and 23, 2009. Reproduced by permission.

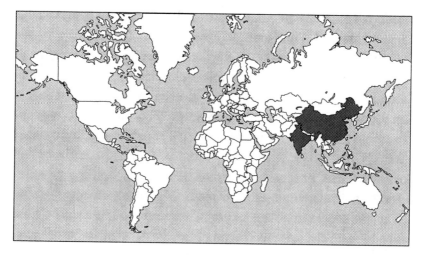

3. In which industries does Donovan say that success was made possible due to freely available research by universities?

India and China face profound, perhaps even existential, economic challenges as they seek to continue providing growth for the hundreds of millions of impoverished citizens who demand economic opportunity and empowerment. As low- and middle-income countries, respectively, the desirability of policies that prove charitable to other countries, especially developed ones, is minimal. Yet, evidence from India shows that intellectual property [IP] enhancement involves the transfer of rents from poor countries to rich ones. Although proponents of increased IP believe the process is mutually advantageous, the small absolute market size of developing countries like India and China does not provide adequate incentives to change the level or direction of total R&D [research and development] expenditure.

Stronger IP Law Helps Others

Intellectual property harmonization actually allows foreign rights holders to capture profits, obtain jobs, decrease the balance of payments, [that essentially lower the trade deficit for foreign countries in relation to India and China] and cause dependency. The anti-competitive, monopolistic nature of intellectual property makes it harder for developing countries to gain access to the most valuable technologies needed for economic convergence. One study showed that even if stronger intellectual property could accelerate FDI [foreign direct investment] it would limit the imitative capability of indigenous firms. Other work found that there is a strong positive effect of intellectual property on domestic imports, leading to a decrease in the balance of payments. Moreover, stronger global IP encourages American exports, something India and China should not necessarily favor. The world's most successful economies, such as Japan or the United States, rose to prominence by specifically limiting the scope and breadth of patents.

The world's most successful economies, such as Japan or the United States, rose to prominence by specifically limiting the scope and breadth of patents.

China and India are countries of enormous internal economic differences, primarily stemming from productivity gaps. The technologies that enable world-class economic efficiency in some parts of China and India need to be diffused throughout the country, but the monopoly pricing associated with IPR [intellectual property rights] limits the ability of the poor to access empowering technology.

IP Is Not Needed for Innovation

Despite the presence of high-tech hubs like Bangalore and Hyderabad, India ranks 63rd out of 72 surveyed countries for the Technology Achievement Index. In China, Beijing and Shanghai have knowledge-intensities 6.1 and 5.3 times the national average, respectively. These disparities indicate an inability to effectively diffuse innovations, likely resulting from the higher prices and protectionism associated with increased intellectual property. The low productivity in most Indian enterprises indicates an enormous opportunity to make better use of existing knowledge; one analysis "implies that the output of the Indian economy could be as much as 4.8 times higher if enterprises were to absorb and use the knowledge that already exists in the economy." Intellectual property is certainly an important factor, but not the only factor preventing this diffusion: after all, India's remarkable agricultural productivity growth known as the Green Revolution took place prior to global intellectual property harmonization.

Even with broadly condemned intellectual property policy, China and India remain highly desirable locations for the R&D labs of major international corporations.

Because R&D requires much more than financial incentives (educated workforce, infrastructure, etc.), close to 80% of global R&D is carried out in the developed world. Therefore, innovation in the developing world is more appropriately adoption and adaptation of existing technology. Instead of hoping that increased intellectual property will attract it (likely a fool's errand), there are other ways to access global knowledge such as reverse engineering, imitation, utilizing diaspora linkages and networks, and simply purchasing knowledge-embodying goods. Even with broadly condemned intellectual property policy, China and India remain highly desirable locations for the R&D tabs of major international corporations. Several surveys indicate that India is the preferred location for innovation centers, likely stemming from the critical mass of low-cost, highly skilled knowledge workers—the average annual salary of a scientist or engineer in India is $22,600, compared to $90,000 in the United States. Additionally, given the ability to digitize and internationally transfer much of their work, India is attractive regardless of concerns about intellectual property infringement. And the benefit to India is impressive:

> "Between 1998 and 2003, MNCs [multinational corporations] made $1.3 billion in R&D investments in India. More than 300 MNCs are setting up R&D and technical centers in India. They employ 80,000 scientists and engineers and spend about $4 billion a year. Planned investment totals $4.7 billion.... The growth of MNC R&D centers generates positive spillovers to the Indian economy." ...

Although MNCs state their preference for higher intellectual property, a recent study noted that "it is unlikely that product patents will make a dramatic difference to their choices"; instead a change in IP will likely most affect domestic firms who are increasing the amount and type of R&D without the incentive of intellectual property. India and China, where a similar trend is present and increasing, can further their attractiveness to FDI through tax breaks, increased liberalization and actively utilizing their diaspora [that is, nationals who have emigrated].

Instead of focusing on intellectual property as the sole source of incentive for innovation, China and India should actively explore and promote ways in which to promote investment in public goods without bringing the distortions of monopoly rights.

Promote Innovation Through Other Means

Stronger intellectual property may also be unnecessary in another way. Although they are promoted as a tool for enhancing economic competitiveness ... their effectiveness is, at most, questionable. ...

Strengthened intellectual property is unlikely to have caused the increase in American patenting in the 1980s: A

Open Source Practices Can Encourage Innovation

[In 2006] an internal science team at a U.S.-based major biotechnology firm was assigned to develop a method for rapid and simple detection of DNA sequences in unconventional field settings. . . . After several months of effort, the team . . . concluded that no viable solution existed for their problem. Since solving the problem was of critical importance for the firm, management decided to break from convention and to disclose the specifics of the problem to a large group of unknown "outside" scientists requesting a solution in return for substantial prize money.

In a four-week period of time, over 574 scientists investigated the problem statement and forty-two of them submitted potential solutions for considerations. The winning solution was proposed by a scientist from Finland who did not work in this field.

Karim R. Lakhani, as told to Martha Lagace,
"Open Source Science: A New Model For Innovation,"
HBS Working Knowledge, *November 20, 2006.*
http://hbswk.hbs.edu.

study of patent reforms over 150 years in 60 countries confirms "that reforms have few positive effects on patent applications by entities based in the country undertaking the policy change." . . .

Instead of focusing on intellectual property as the sole source of incentive for innovation, China and India should actively explore and promote ways in which to promote investment in public goods without bringing the distortions of monopoly rights. As legal scholar [Lawrence] Lessig writes in *The Future of Ideas: The Fate of the Commons in a Connected*

World, "There is no necessity to marry the incentive to innovate to conferral of monopoly power in innovations." Digital, networked technology expands the ability for people to collaborate across time and space, significantly decreasing the up-front costs of innovation that intellectual property seeks to recuperate through exclusive rights. Models of open source [practices that allow users to access software source codes] innovation have proven spectacularly successful in software development where innovation is a cumulative and competitive process. Open licensing models also hold promise in biotechnology where much of the research costs are provided by academic researchers who have an interest in promoting knowledge widely. In fact, IT [information technology] and biotechnology were successful in large part due to the freely available research made possible by university knowledge. Funding can also be provided by nonprofit entities such as government-awarded prizes for socially desirable innovations. Finally, even in a market without intellectual property, large up-front costs associated with innovation can be recouped through trade secrecy and the first-mover advantage [that is, by the fact that the first producer to enter a market has an advantage].

Poland's Copyright Laws Allow Sampling

Tomasz Rychlicki and Adam Zielinski

Tomasz Rychlicki and Adam Zielinski are Polish lawyers specializing in intellectual property cases. In the following viewpoint, the authors note that many musicians use sampling in Poland, but that few court cases involving sampling have been tried in the courts. The authors argue that Polish law provides for a right of quotation and that sampling could be considered quotation in many instances. As a result, the authors believe Polish artists could sample as long as they credit the original source, even if they do not obtain permission to do so.

As you read, consider the following questions:

1. Why did Rihanna's song "Please Don't Stop the Music" run afoul of copyright law?
2. What is the definition of derived works under Polish law, according to the authors?
3. Why do the authors believe that their opinions about sampling in Polish law may spark controversy?

Have you ever turned on the radio, heard a song for the first time, and thought there was something vaguely familiar about parts of it? Well, you may have been listening to what today is termed "sampling." Over the last couple of de-

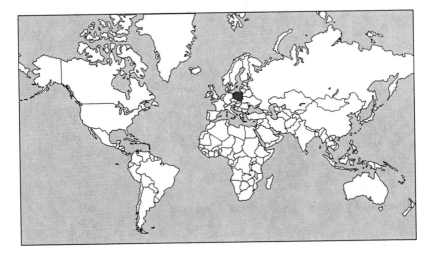

cades, it has become an increasingly popular way to make music. Sampling is simply the extraction of fragments from existing musical works, which are used in the composition of creative, new pieces. One can immediately see why it has engendered a number of copyright litigation cases.

One example that caught the headlines earlier this year [2009] was the hit song "Please Don't Stop the Music" by Rihanna. Parts of the song had been sampled from Michael Jackson's 1983 hit "Wanna Be Startin' Something" for which Rihanna claims she sought his permission. However, it turns out that Jackson had, himself, sampled that fragment from "Soul Makossa," by Afro funk jazzman Manu Dibango from Cameroon. First recorded in 1972, it is considered by many to be the first disco song. Manu Dibango, now 75 years old, is suing both Jackson and Rihanna for copyright infringement in the French courts.

The United States vs. Poland

The U.S., the cradle of sampling, also saw the birth of the first music sampling litigation cases. In [the 1991] federal court case *Grand Upright Music Limited v. Warner Bros. Records Inc.*, the judge began his sentence with a biblical quote—"thou shalt not steal." He then granted an injunction to Grand Up-right Music to prevent further copyright infringement of the Gilbert O'Sullivan song "Alone Again" by Warner Bros. Records, whose signed artist, rapper Biz Markie, had sampled it in a track on his *I Need a Haircut* album. The quote was symbolic of the way in which U.S. courts would thereafter deal with sampling. The decision changed the *modus operandi* of the hip-hop music industry which, from then on, had to ensure all music sampling was preapproved by copyright owners.

The authors of this [viewpoint] ask: Are there legal arguments that could enable courts to decide differently on sampling? This [viewpoint] discusses the possibilities by analyzing the current situation in Poland.

Sampling is common in Poland, and not just with rappers. Some artists who sample seek, and are granted, approval from the original authors; others turn a blind eye to this requirement. The music industry has been effective in discouraging cases involving sampling from being taken to court. As a result, there has been little development of Polish case law on sampling. If even a shadow of a dispute threatens to arise, the parties manage to swiftly reach an agreement.

Sampling is common in Poland and not just with rappers.

Consider the following hypotheses, which fall well within the boundaries of the Polish law on authors' rights and related rights:

- Can sampled works be considered derived works?

- Can sampled works be considered new works based on the right of quotation?

Derivation and Quotation

Polish law does not use terms such as "sample" or "sampling." It does, however, define derived works (derivatives), which are understood to be transformations or adaptations of existing works bearing features of originality, creativity and individuality. Authors of derivative works intending to disseminate their creations need the consent of the author of the original work.

Works that feature sampling, therefore, can be deemed derived works containing elements of artistic works taken from an original source, but they are, nevertheless, the creative works of their makers. In which case, the original author should be mentioned as the creator/author along with the creator of the new work, and the derivative work must cite the name of the original track that was sampled. A derived work encapsulates both the creative features of an original work and the innovative endeavors of another person, and both must be recognized.

If that is the case, could the sampling in the U.S. cases . . . be considered derived works? Apart from significant departures from statutory requirements—non-recognition of the author and title and, above all, failure to seek the consent of the original author—in most cases, probably yes. If so, however, should all cases of sampling be considered derived works? In our opinion—no! Here is why.

New works containing samples as part of the creative work of an artist . . . could be recognized as cases of lawful quotation.

Article 29, paragraph 1 of the Polish law on authors' rights provides for the possibility that authors and creators may quote other works: "It shall be permissible to reproduce in the form of quotations, in works that constitute an integral whole, fragments of disclosed works or the entire contents of short works to the extent justified by explanation, critical analysis or

Brazil Experiments with Reducing Restrictions on Music

Late one tropical evening last year [2003], a small delegation of American online-rights activists and scholars—including Stanford's Lawrence Lessig, Harvard's William Fisher, and John Perry Barlow of the Electronic Frontier Foundation—sat in the living room of a beachfront Rio de Janeiro penthouse, preaching the virtues of Internet-powered cultural sharing to Brazil's newly appointed minister of culture. The minister himself, Gilberto Gil, sat on the floor, cross-legged and barefoot, cradling an acoustic guitar in his lap. In addition to being one of Brazil's most high-profile politicians, Gil is also one of its biggest pop stars, with almost four decades of classic back catalog to his name. It was unclear, therefore, just how Gil would respond to the Americans' pitch: an online music archive that might one day contain every Brazilian song ever recorded, all downloadable for free. . . .

As it turned out, Gil was happy to give the project his backing. A few months later, he agreed to lend the government's imprimatur to a new digital-sampling license designed by Creative Commons, the US nonprofit founded by Lessig to explore alternatives to the increasingly restrictive terms of copyright. What's more, Gil had also agreed to . . . rerelease a handful of his own classic hits under the new license, free for anyone to slice, dice, and spice up their creations with, a few seconds at a time.

Julian Dibbell,
"We Pledge Allegiance to the Penguin,"
Wired, *November 2004. www.wired.com.*

teaching or by the characteristics of the kind of creativity concerned." By extrapolation, new works containing samples as part of the creative work of an artist—but that are not simply mixes and remixes of other works—could be recognized as cases of lawful quotation.

In other words, a work created in such a way could be recognized as an independent work incorporating quotations. An example of a musical quotation from the "pre-sampling" era would be a musical variation—defined as a work "referring to a subject, motif or another work" and the result of "a creative processing of that work." In which case, creative sampling can be recognized as an activity justified by the type of works involved and, by the same token, fulfilling the Article 29 requirement. This signifies that, to avoid a charge of plagiarism, the author or original artist and source of the work must be mentioned—but not necessarily in the title—without the need to seek permission, the quotation right being a statutory license.

Creative freedom, such as sampling, can, and should, be defended and treated as a part of the progress of art.

No Copyright Infringement

The above arguments regarding the Polish law on authors' rights may well spark controversy, since sampling has never been extensively covered in Polish case law or legal and academic analyses. But it is the legal opinion of the authors that sampling does not constitute copyright infringement if the right of quotation is properly executed.

There is of course an enormous difference between the cheap plagiarism understood by some as "derivative works," and the original and creative endeavor in which samples form a starting point for creating new works that could fall under the "right of quotation" rule rather than be considered derivative works. Each case requires thorough, individual analysis. But creative freedom, such as sampling, can, and should, be defended and treated as a part of the progress of art, which, in turn, furthers the development and enrichment of human culture.

Video Game Piracy Can Teach Game Manufacturers Important Lessons

Paul Wiedel

Paul Wiedel is a Minneapolis writer and blogger who works in the computer software industry. In the following viewpoint, he argues that pirated video games are successful in part because they are fast, free, and safe, and so provide a better retail experience than do legal sellers. Sellers should therefore learn from pirates in order to provide a better experience for consumers. In particular, Wiedel suggests that companies should distribute games online rather than through retail outlets and that they should provide support or multiplayer opportunities that are not available to those with pirated copies.

As you read, consider the following questions:

1. What questions about piracy does Wiedel believe are a waste of time to try to answer?
2. According to Wiedel, why are most video game purchases regrettable?
3. What is the best software companies can hope to do in terms of preventing piracy, according to Wiedel?

Paul Wiedel, "Making Video Game Piracy Obsolete," *Intellectual Detritus*, September 29, 2008. Reproduced by permission of the author.

Video game piracy, and intellectual property piracy is one of the most polarizing and complex issues that I have faced. People hold strong opinions on piracy that are all over the spectrum. There are people who want to see pirates thrown in jail and all their assets seized. There are people who believe that piracy is every person's God given right. There are those who pirate as a means of trying before they buy.

Learn to Love the Pirates

What's interesting is that on both sides of the argument are claims that the other side is wrong. Instead of fighting with each other, why not cooperate? Most people who use pirated games don't want to steal, and well, I don't know about game sellers, they seem to really hate pirates. But I think they should learn to love them.

Most people who use pirated games don't want to steal, and well, I don't know about game sellers, they seem to really hate pirates. But I think they should learn to love them.

There are a ton of questions that people have difficulty answering when it comes to piracy:

Is piracy stealing?

Is piracy morally wrong?

Is piracy worse than shoplifting?

Is piracy ever justifiable?

Is expending energy answering these questions a waste of time?

I don't know the answer to any but the last question and I say yes to that.

The more interesting questions to me [are]: Why do people pirate and how can its damaging effects be minimized? Let me ask an even better question: Can piracy be beneficial to the gaming industry?

My top three answers to the first question are piracy is fast, piracy is free, and piracy is safe. My answer to the last question, I will answer way at the end. . . . But first, I will discuss why I believe piracy is so prolific and how its destructive effects can be minimized.

Fast, Free, and Safe

Consider Ubuntu Linux [an operating system distributed online for free]. I can download the entire contents of a CD for Ubuntu Linux in a few minutes with BitTorrent [an Internet protocol or system for distributing large amounts of data]. The speed with which I can get content via that protocol makes it a superior and preferable option to any other form of distribution. Pirates use the same protocol to distribute content. They do it because it is the most efficient means available. If something better were to come along, they would adopt it immediately. There is a lot one can learn from pirates.

"If it's free, I want it."—a buddy of mine from college. That buddy ended up having an apartment full of crap, but he has an interesting point. Free, as a price point, is difficult to beat. In the current paradigm of video game commerce, a pirate can easily get a game that is better than the one they could buy at a store for free.

It's safe. There is virtually no perceived risk in piracy. Not counting computer viruses or litigation, there isn't much of a risk involved in software piracy. If you don't like it, you delete it and you go about your business. There are two interesting effects of this risk-free environment: People try out new products at will, and it creates a really good picture of what kinds of products people like.

Compare piracy with buying a software 'the right way'.

Retail purchases of games require some form of waiting, either waiting for the game to be delivered via the mail or making a trip to a B&M store. Take my own situation for example. I live within 2 miles of a Target and within 5 miles of a Best Buy and a GameStop. Getting to a store and back isn't a big deal. If I really want a game now, I can probably get one within 15 minutes. 15 minutes that I would need to spend going to and from a store in my car to pick up a game. 15 minutes that I could have spent doing any number of other things, just so I could pick up a game. Compare that to getting a game online, I can just pick something out and let my computer do the work while I'm off doing whatever it is that I do.

Buying games through retail is expensive. It's expensive not only in terms of time, but also money. Some games sell for as much as $60. That's half a week of food for my wife and me. That's a tank of gas. That's two rounds of golf at my local golf course. All of those things are what I'm comparing your product to when I decide whether I'm going to buy it. Is your product comparable to going out to dinner with friends? The $60 price point is something I would need to really think about, and I'd probably get my butt kicked by my wife if I bought a $60 game without telling her. For $30, I can pick that up without getting my butt kicked.

Price points become important when you consider the risks of buying a game. If you pay $60 for a game that sucks, well you just wasted $60. I don't know of a retailer that will accept a return on a game. They learned that a lot of people return video games. Why? The two reasons that seem obvious are: 1) the game sucks, or 2) the customer is tired of it. In both cases the customers did not feel that they received sufficient value for their money.

Antipiracy advocates always talk about how the people who make the games work hard. Customers work equally as hard for their money and they don't want to feel ripped off and cheated. Sound familiar? Just because you work hard to create a product doesn't mean that you are entitled to sales. If I plow sand, it's going to be a lot of work. When it comes time to harvest the fruits of my work there isn't going to be much. Is it anyone else's fault that I picked a poor spot to farm?

So, what is the problem? Piracy is able to compete with the traditional retail paradigm by ways of speed, risk, and price. By pirating software, people are able to enjoy the same experiences without any of the negative effects of the traditional retail experience.

By pirating software, people are able to enjoy the same experiences without any of the negative effects of the traditional retail experience.

How to Compete with Pirates

The only way to eliminate the effects of piracy is to make it obsolete, or better yet, make it work for you. I propose the following plan to compete with piracy on the basis of speed, risk, and value.

1. Compete on the basis of speed. Digital distribution is the way of the future. Look at Steam [a digital distribution system used to distribute games online]. They are doing a lot of things right. Steam is my preferred point of purchase for video games because they mitigate many of the downsides of purchasing video games. Digital distribution is competing directly with piracy in terms of speed.

Printing physical media is a waste of resources and a wasteful practice. Instead of treating your products like a physical good, treat it exclusively as a license. When a person purchases a license treat it as a key to use your product. Look at how Steam and most MMOs [massively multiplayer online games, which support hundreds or thousands of players at once] work. You can download the software through the publisher's site easily and quickly. You just need an account in good standing to play the game.

It costs way less to distribute digitally than it does to manufacture a physical product and distribute that physical product via traditional logistics. It is also, largely unnecessary.

2. Mitigate the risk of purchasing your product. Take a minute to look at how video game publishers work. Let's face facts and admit that most video game purchases are regrettable.

Why is this? I think the biggest reason is because games are pushed out to market before they reach an acceptable level of maturity. Add to this the level of support that people receive after they purchase a game, typically zero, and it is easy to see why people feel cheated or ripped off when they make the mistake of buying a game.

Instead of abandoning your customer with your incomplete mess of a game, why not stand by your work? Are you in the business of deceiving people into buying your product and then ditching them once you have cash in hand or are you in the business of creating and selling a high-quality experience to your customers? If your customers feel that you are trying to rip them off, there are many potential customers who will not hesitate to rip you off instead.

Do the right thing, if you sell crap, buck up and take responsibility for your bad product. If you feel entitled to your customer's money because they were unfortunate enough to believe your marketing and you treat them as such, do you think that the same people will hesitate to feel entitled to receive everything you ever did or will create for free because they paid for a piece of incomplete and malfunctioning garbage? Pirates aren't the only ones who feel entitled to the fruits of others' hard work.

Respect your customer and they will respect you. Look at Blizzard [Entertainment, manufacturer of *Warcraft* and *Starcraft*, and other game series]. Nobody will accuse them of selling crap. They can't meet a deadline to save their lives, but their work is excellent. They are the pinnacle of video game developers. People do not hesitate to purchase Blizzard products. When *Diablo III* hits the shelves there will be people lining up to buy it. Yes, people will want to pirate it too, but the vast majority of them will want to buy it because Blizzard will . . .

Respect your customer and they will respect you.

---

3. Make the gaming experience for the purchased product vastly better than the experience that a pirated product can give. A few ways in which this can be accommodated are to provide an enhanced online experience—people with pirated products will be hesitant to use . . . a game maker's servers with a pirated product. If they aren't, well you know where to send the bill. Look at the MMO games that have a subscription-based model, piracy isn't a big problem with them, because running a pirated product isn't very useful. It's actually in a subscription-based service's best interest to allow people to distribute their products on their own. It reduces the bandwidth load . . . more on that later.

I think the software developing world could learn a lot from Blizzard. They don't sell any product until it reaches their high standards. They continue to offer a fantastic online experience with their titles well after their products sell. Look at *Starcraft*, it has been on the market for 10 years. During that time, its use has shifted focus from the single player game to the online game play [where large numbers of people interact on Blizzard's platform], which is provided by Blizzard for no additional charge.

Providing the server for no additional charge makes sense in my opinion. The game seller can control who uses their product online. By controlling the online game, the game seller can control who uses it, i.e., keep the pirates out. They can also provide a better experience than the pirated version.

Countries with the Largest Percentage of Pirated Game Download by Volume, 2009

Country	Percentage
Italy	20.3
Spain	12.5
France	7.5
Brazil	6
China	5.7

Tom Ivan, "ESA: Game Piracy Highest in Europe,"
Edge, February 19, 2010. www.next-gen.biz.

I believe that too many game publishers are spending too many resources trying to make game piracy impossible. I'm going to let you guys in on a little secret, it is a loser's game. Most game security professionals will tell you that at best you can hope to make it difficult enough for the pirated version to only be ubiquitous after the game launches [rather than before the game comes out]. Instead of spending resources trying to fight a losing battle, why not use your enemies' forces to work for you.

Instead of calculating a pirated copy as a potential loss of purchase, why not treat it as a potential sale?

Turn Pirates into Customers

The million-dollar question is how to turn what some claim is destroying the video game industry into something that helps it. The key is simple, provide a better experience through the purchased product than a pirated version can deliver. That is to say, give the person you call a pirate a compelling reason to become the person you call a customer.

Instead of calculating a pirated copy as a potential loss of purchase, why not treat it as a potential sale? Instead of turning a list of pirates over to legal, why not turn that list over to sales? There is no way to 'win' with a lawyer, it's just a degree of loss.

Instead of turning them into martyrs and your peers into monsters, turn the people who have tried your product out a chance to become paying customers. You don't need Ricky Roma [a salesman in the play and movie *Glengarry Glen Ross*] to come in and schmooze someone into a sale, they know your product. Even better than knowing your product, they already have it, anything you gain from them is pure profit.

Engineer the product so it isn't all that challenging to be 'pirated' as a product that is inferior to what the purchased version can deliver. Online multiplayer is just an example, another strategy that can work is to provide extra downloadable content at no extra charge to paying customers. Engineer the product so that 'pirating' it is not much different than distributing a good demo. It wasn't long ago that companies like id [Software, the company that created the game *Doom*] and Blizzard offered rich playable demos of games like *Doom*, *Quake*, and *Warcraft*. I don't know what ever happened to those franchises, but I do know that we played the crap out of them in college and spread the word about how awesome those games are.

Learn to live with piracy. It's going to happen.

What else is piracy good for? Market research. Torrent numbers [the number of people currently downloading a product] on certain notorious Web sites based in Scandinavian countries [the Pirate Bay, a major pirate Web site based in Sweden] don't need to be insulting. They're performing a few services to the content-producing community. They are showing what people are interested in. The more people who torrent a title is pretty significant. Yes it doesn't directly translate into sales, but it does show what people want when cost is not a factor. That's information that is ripe for the taking. If you read the threads about the games, you can see what people honestly think about the games. They didn't pay anything for it, so they aren't going to be nearly as hostile or angry as a disappointed paying customer.

Lastly, learn to live with piracy. It's going to happen and no matter what technical and legal means are used to try and stop it altogether, there will be some who will take it as a challenge to defeat those countermeasures. Make it easy on yourselves, develop strategies to use piracy to your benefit, and then you can focus on the things that you really want to focus on.

Periodical Bibliography

The following articles have been selected to supplement the diverse views presented in this chapter.

Julian Dibbell   "We Pledge Allegiance to the Penguin," *Wired*, November 2004. www.wired.com.

Kevin Donovan   "The Way Forward on Intellectual Property for China and India," Techdirt Blog, September 3, 2009. www.techdirt.com.

Economist   "China, America and Intellectual Property: A Tale of Two iPhones," February 9, 2010. www.economist.com.

Howard W. French   "China Media Battle Hints at Shift on Intellectual Property," *New York Times*, January 6, 2007. www.nytimes.com.

Kembrew McLeod   "How to Make a Documentary About Sampling—Legally," *Atlantic*, March 31, 2010. www.theatlantic.com.

Jonathan Newman   "Steal This Blog," Hooded Utilitarian Blog, March 12, 2010. www.tcj.com./ hoodedutilitarian.

JR Raphael   "The Pirate Bay Verdict and the Future of File Sharing," *PCWorld*, April 17, 2009. www.pcworld.com.

Simon Reynolds   "What Is Your Sampling Epiphany?" Guardian .co.uk, February 26, 2009. www.guardian.co.uk.

Shane Richmond   "Will the Pirate Party Manifesto Influence the Intellectual Property Debate?" Telegraph.co.uk, March 24, 2010. http://blogs.telegraph.co.uk.

CHAPTER 3

Popular Culture and Censorship

In Iran, Technology Is Subverting Censorship of Western Pop Culture

Manal Lutfi

Manal Lutfi writes regularly for Asharq Al-Awsat, *an Arabic international daily newspaper. She is also the lead author of* Human Rights Guarantees Under the Palestinian Self-Rule Authority. *In the following viewpoint, she argues that satellite dishes, personal computers, and other technological advances have made it possible for many Iranians to experience Western music, film, and culture despite government bans. For similar reasons, Iranians are also increasingly able to make and distribute their own music, music videos, and films. Despite sensorship, therefore, Iranians actually have access to a wide variety of popular culture.*

As you read, consider the following questions:

1. According to Lutfi, why do the vast majority of Iranians choose to own satellite dishes?

2. How many Internet users did Iran have in 1993, and how many did it have in 2007, according to Lutfi?

3. Mohammad Biran, a worker in a DVD shop in Tehran, says that most banned films come into Iran by what route?

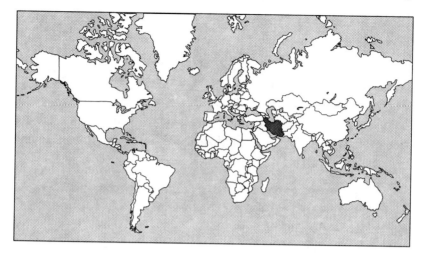

"15 years ago, whoever purchased a cassette player would wrap it up and hide it in the car so that no one would discover it. The same thing applied to satellite dishes, but now it is normal to own one," explained Armeni, a young middle-class Iranian, as he commented on the changes that had been introduced gradually over the past ten years in Iranian society.

Two Worlds

In Iran, items that are banned are readily available locally. These include satellite dishes, certain types of music, films, books and Web sites, in addition to certain types of clothing. For everything that is officially banned, there is an illegal alternative, for example, there are thousands of Web sites that have been blocked by the Iranian authorities; however, many young Iranians are technologically savvy and can bypass the country's censors. There are also many films that are subjected to censorship or are banned in some cases, but at the same time these films are available in Iran and uncut versions can be found. Also certain genres of music like hip-hop are prohibited but they are popular amongst the Iranian youth and can be heard from cars as youngsters drive around the city at night. There are two worlds in Iran that contradict each other yet exist side by side.

Armeni owns a car and every summer, he travels to a European country to spend the holidays. Approximately 90% of Iranians have satellite receivers in their homes but this does not mean that official restrictions on buying satellite receivers have changed in Iran over the past few years.

There are two worlds in Iran that contradict each other yet exist side by side.

Arsh Ferhadi, a business journalist told *Asharq Al-Awsat*, "Journalists, doctors, publishers, officials and university professors can easily obtain a license from the Ministry of Culture and Islamic Guidance to install satellite receivers. As for other Iranians, they must give a plausible reason to want to buy a satellite dish. After this, the ministry considers the request and makes a decision. The majority of people prefer to avoid this procedure and purchase satellite dishes and install them without getting permission". The overwhelming majority of Iranians, regardless of their economic or educational level or piousness, owns satellite dishes, as it is the only alternative to official media in Iran. The official Iranian radio and television are subject to direct supervision from the Supreme Leader Ayatollah Ali Khamenei. Besides the eight official stations in Iran that include a Quran channel, a news channel and a sports channel, there are foreign channels that are legally permitted such as Aljazeera [an Arabic network], BBC channels and the Euronews channel in French. Nevertheless, there are no private television channels in Iran. Due to Iranian television's affiliation to the Supreme Guide, programs, films and series are subject to strict criteria, the majority of which are religious or social. Many young people regard these channels as traditional and conservative besides that they do not reflect the changes that take place in Iran. For example, neckties have been considered "taboo" since the Iranian Revolution in 1979 [when a Muslim revolution overthrew a Western-backed secular government], based on the fact that they are Western symbols and a reference to the "Westernized" class of technocrats. Therefore, neckties are not worn today in Iran and do not appear in television programs or films except in reference to evil characters that in most cases are from the era of the Shah [the leader overthrown by the 1979 Iranian Revolution]. But as part of everyday life, some Iranians who belong to the middle class wear neckties at weddings or in private parties generally.

The former president of Iran, Mohammad Khatami, sought to expand the scope of social freedoms and allowed music concerts to be broadcast and the playing of traditional musical instruments such as the sitar and tambour to be aired during his term. This was considered a calm cultural revolution, taking into account that it was the first time that live concerts were broadcast and that musical instruments were shown on television since the Iranian Revolution. However, the steps taken during Khatami's presidency began to recede; the current [2007] Iranian Minister of Guidance and Culture, Mohammad-Hossein Saffar-Harandi, has a negative opinion of music. When he assumed his post, he stated that one of the first issues that he would combat would be the types of music that are against the values of the Republic of Iran, including rock and rap. He called upon Iranian musicians to produce purposeful and meaningful music, thus some of them produced a "nuclear symphony" that supports Iran's right to develop a nuclear program for peaceful purposes. Even though there is an opera house in Iran, its activities are limited to hosting foreign groups that play classical music or Spanish musicians owing to the great popularity of Spanish music in Iran. However, such events take place only every now and again.

Music Is Available Online

Many young people, such as Armeni, have solved the problem of music. Armeni now spends a lot of his free time watching and listening to music and music videos on his personal computer in his room. Such is the black market for music, which makes significant profits and the popularity of which increased during the presidency of Khatami, who was unable to grant music a fully legal status but at the same time allowed it to spread freely.

The real music business is underground, the products of which are discreetly manufactured.

Armeni told *Asharq Al-Awsat*, "Music that is sold openly in stores does not represent the music business in Iran. The real music business is underground, the products of which are discretely manufactured. The transactions of this kind of music outnumber the number of transactions of legal music." Owing to the fact that television does not broadcast concerts, songs or music video clips, underground music (or Zirzamin in Persian) has become the way of entertainment that is not subject to supervision. Armeni added, "Those who produce and write this music are very talented artists. They want to say things and express their thoughts and ideas on issues through banned music. What do they do? They sit together and produce music and then they copy the tape and either do not put names on them or they use an alias. The tapes are then sent to be sold illegally. We promote the music amongst ourselves by telling other people about the song and where it is available. There are Iranians living in Los Angeles who try to produce music and sell it here but it is not as good or as moving as music that is made in Iran."

Underground Fame

In Iran today, there are many young bands, some of which use classical poetry mixed with rock music. Modern Iranian music is now a mixture of a Western style and a local flavor through the use of Iranian instruments such as the tanbur and sitar. Some popular acts for this style of music include Reza Yazdani, Ali Lohrasbi and Zir Khat Fajr, a rap group whose latest album is called *Poverty Line*. Themes of songs include love, poverty, frustration and loneliness.

Only a moderate budget is needed to produce an underground music video as many of them are filmed in the homes of the music artists where the singer will dance to his/her music.

O-Hum is another popular Iranian band, specializing in rock music, who were allowed to stage a concert (nonsegregated) for the Christian minority in Iran during Christmas celebrations. The band calls its style "Persian Rock" because it mixes classical Iranian music (using the tambour and sitar) with rock music. O-Hum was formed in 1999 by Shahram Sharbaf, Babak Riahipour and Shahrokh Izadkhah. Their plan was to record a few demos at Shahram's house but the first song that was recorded was circulated until it reached a music company in Tehran that then signed the band to a record contract. After the album was recorded, it was sent to the Iranian Ministry of Culture and Islamic Guidance to be cleared for release. However, the ministry refused this and said that the album is nothing but "tacky Western music" that conflicts with Islamic principles and values. This led to the record company cancelling the contract and dropping the band. O-Hum decided to launch its own Web site and uploaded all its songs on to the Internet to be downloaded by the public free. A few months after the launch of the Web site, the band became one of the most popular underground groups in Iran. The group encouraged other musicians to produce music and sell it over the Internet that is not subjected to government supervision. The Internet made O-Hum and other groups famous in Iran and among Iranians abroad as well as among foreigners interested in Iranian music. A track by the band titled "Hafez in Love" was downloaded 15,000 times in its first week of release.

In addition, "underground" music videos are also being produced and are enjoying increasing popularity. Only a moderate budget is needed to produce an underground music video as many of them are filmed in the homes of the music artists where the singer will dance to his/her music. In concerts that are permitted by the authorities, singers and spectators are not allowed to dance to music. The Internet has led to a revolution in the Iranian music industry and despite the numerous Web sites that have been blocked by Iranian authorities, especially pornographic sites or Web sites of opponents to the regime who reside outside of the country, Iran has approximately 10 million Internet users [in 2007]. This number could rise to 25 million by 2009 from 1 million users in 1993. Many Internet users have knowledge on how to decipher these prohibited Web sites, but what is notable is that they are not primarily interested in politics as much as they are interested in music, films and books. As much as official music is subject to restrictions by the Iranian Ministry of Culture and Islamic Guidance, the same applies to films.

Underground Film

From the beginning stage, the concept of a film must be approved by the Ministry of Culture and Islamic Guidance. In this regard Iranian filmmaker Saifullah Dad, who was the adviser in charge of cinema during Khatami's term, told *Asharq Al-Awsat*, "I heard that over the past few years, since the new government came into power, the issue of the film industry is a little more challenging. During Khatami's presidency, we would give permission to directors without even reading the plot of the film. This has changed now as restrictive procedures have been reintroduced within the ministry. If you want

Private and Public Culture in Iran

In [Iran,] a land where paradoxes abound, the division that exists between the interior and exterior, between the private and public spheres is just one of many. The separation of these domains has created a dualism that has become inherent in Iranian culture and a defining feature of most artistic endeavours in Iran. In the outside world, the sense of social decorum must be upheld with utmost vigour. In the outside world, women wear the *hejab* [a veil that covers the head and neck of a Muslim woman]. In the outside world, art, whether painting or poetry, is communicated through a veil of abstraction as artists attempt to elude the critical eye of censors.

But once indoors, veils can be discarded, rap, rock and pop can be blasted from stereos, hips can sway, banned poetry can be recited, prohibited literature read, forbidden films watched and art of any kind can adorn the walls.

Article 19: Global Campaign for Free Expression,
"Unveiled: Art and Censorship in Iran,"
September 2006. www.article19.org.

to make a film you have to go to the Ministry of Culture and Islamic Guidance with a brief plot of about ten pages. If it is approved, then you hand them the final script in full. If they agree to it, then you can get permission to start filming. These initial steps do not necessarily mean that the Ministry of Culture and Islamic Guidance will delete or disapprove of parts of the film, but it implies that the ministry is inevitably informed about the films that are currently produced". Today and for reasons related to production and censorship, the works of many Iranian directors, such as Abbas Kiarostami [director of *Taste of Cherry*], have decreased significantly.

However, some people do not consider this a big problem and they believe that censorship exists in varying degrees in all societies and that there are benefits to it. They argue that Iranian directors who are financed from abroad can exaggerate and present incorrect information about the conditions in Iran and rather reflect the perspectives that Western states that fund them want to focus on.

An Iranian university professor, who spoke to *Asharq Al-Awsat* on condition of anonymity told *Asharq Al-Awsat*, "Do not think that directors such as Mohsen Makhmalbaf [director of *Sex & Philosophy*] and his daughter Samira Makhmalbaf enjoy any kind of popularity in Iran as some may imagine. They have not lived in Iran for a while now. They direct films that defame the country at a very critical time. Who funds their films? The French and other Western parties fund them. I do not think that this is the enlightening or educational role of cinema. There are other Iranian directors living in Iran and directing films under the current circumstances and they are much better."

As for foreign films showing in Iran, whether in cinemas or on television, these are usually social or "action" films that are imported from China, Japan and Malaysia and all of them are dubbed into Farsi [the main language in Iran]. All of these films should first be presented to the Ministry of Culture and Islamic Guidance, to ensure their compatibility with the Islamic standards of Iran (only foreign women are allowed to appear without head scarves). Iranian television sometimes airs American films but they are not publicized as American films, according to an Iranian activist who told *Asharq Al-Awsat*, "Sometimes the story is changed, for example, if the story is about a co-habiting couple, in the Persian translation, the couple would be married."

A number of Iranian cinemas, including Bahman and Farhang are located near Tehran University, however the films that are screened there are not diverse enough according to many young people. Action films and films based on comics are the most popular films in Iran. The markets for videos and DVDs that are smuggled into Iran are the alternative [to cinema] and offer all newly released films from all over the world, especially America. However, these films are not subject to censorship, like the other films that are examined by the Ministry of Culture and Islamic Guidance. This is a great advantage that is appreciated only after comparing a censored version of a film. These shops that sell DVDs do not fail in obtaining copies of any films from *Schindler's List* [from 1993] that follows the tragedies of the Jews during the Holocaust to *The Nativity Story* [from 2006, about the birth of Jesus]. Prices of films range from one to two dollars. Mohammed Biran, a young Iranian working in one of the DVD shops in northern Tehran, said that the majority of banned films come from Malaysia and are smuggled into Pakistan and cross the border into Iran via Zahedan [a city in southeastern Iraq].

Videos and DVDs that are smuggled into Iran ... offer all newly released films from all over the world, especially America.

Richness and Diversity

In addition to music and movies, books enjoy widespread popularity in Iran. There are over 40,000 titles printed in Iran each year, most of which are literature and poetry. The majority of these books are translations of major Western writers and poets. As one walks around Inqilab Square, the square of libraries in Tehran, one will find the library shelves stacked with the works of Karl Marx, Vladimir Lenin, Leon Trotsky, Che Guevara, William Shakespeare, Samuel Beckett, Virginia Woolf, [Franz] Kafka, Dstowski, Mario Vargas, Argun, [Johann Wolfgang von] Goethe, Sigmund Freud and Henrik Ibsen. Ilham, a young Iranian woman who lived in Canada for a while before returning to Tehran said, "Iran is an open and diverse society but this is not portrayed in the media. Iranian society is like a watermelon, it looks dry on the surface but on the inside there is richness and diversity."

Thailand Should Not Censor Films on Controversial Issues

Lynette Lee Corporal

Lynette Lee Corporal is a journalist and an editor for news agency Inter Press Service (IPS) Asia-Pacific. In the following viewpoint, she reports that Thailand is moving away from a system of outright bans and toward a system of film rating. However, the new law still allows for censoring and banning of certain films. The censorship of a Japanese-Thai production, Children of the Dark, *about child sex slavery, highlights the difficulty of confronting important issues in film in Thailand.*

As you read, consider the following questions:

1. Who received censorship power under the Film Act of 1930 in Thailand?
2. Into what languages was the documentary by MTV EXIT translated?
3. What are some taboos during media coverage of child trafficking, according to ECPAT media guidelines?

It's film festival time [October 2008] in the Thai capital, but many movie enthusiasts still feel, well, left in the dark by the recent banning of the Japanese-Thai film *Children of the Dark*, which was deemed too sensitive by the authorities.

Lynette Lee Corporal, "Thailand: Film Censorship Leaves Viewers in the Dark," Asia Media Forum, October 21, 2008. Reproduced by permission.

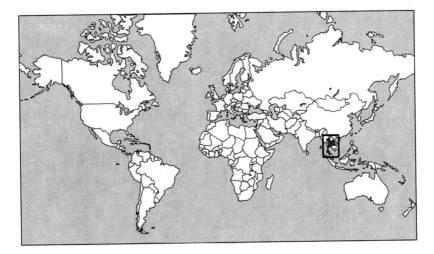

Laws Change, but Censorship Remains

This is especially in the wake of the new film act, which favours a rating system over making cuts in films.

The feature film *Children of the Dark*, which is about child sex slavery, never saw the light of day at the 2008 Bangkok International Film Festival on Sep 23–30, 2008, because Thai censors—via a statement released by festival officials—deemed that it was 'inappropriate' and touched on a 'sensitive' issue.

The ban puts under the spotlight the country's—or at least its higher-ups—seeming unwillingness to let go of the Film Act of 1930, when Thailand was still under absolute monarchy. That law gave a board of censors the power to impose cuts or to ban a film it deems inappropriate. Apart from officials of the Royal Thai Police and the Ministry of Culture, the board gets advice and input from the religious community, academe and other sectors.

In April 2007, the internationally acclaimed Thai film, *Syndromes and a Century*, was withdrawn from commercial release in Thailand by its director Apichatpong Weerasethakul after censors demanded that several scenes be cut. In April

2008, the film was shown on a limited run, with the censored scenes replaced by black patches as the director's way of protesting the censorship.

But on Dec. 20 that year, the new Film and Video Act of 2007 became law, due to take effect in October 2008. Unlike the earlier film act, this new law promotes instead the ratings of films into several categories. Still, critics are unhappy with the fact that films can still be subjected to censorship or an outright ban if they are found "to undermine or disrupt social order and moral decency, or might impact national security or the pride of the nation".

"Authorities always think that viewers need to be protected and shielded from real issues. They still have that kind of sentiment that the media should function as a gatekeeper. That is, let the good stories in and the bad ones out. It's okay in certain circumstances but not when talking about real, serious issues," Thai documentary filmmaker Pipope Panitchpakdi told AMF [Asia Media Forum] in a phone interview.

"Authorities always think that viewers need to be protected and shielded from real issues."

No Kissing

"This country has no problem with hypocrisy; we don't see anything wrong with double standards. We have sex workers in corners of the city, but we can't watch people kissing," said Pipope. "If you do a film about Cambodia now, it's most likely to be banned. It is all about relativism to the extreme," he added, referring to the volatile situation that Thailand and neighbouring Cambodia are in now due to the disputed Preah Vihear Temple at their border.

In his blog, a Bangkok-based journalist who calls himself Wise Kwai, questioned the banning and stated that "the old ways still cling" and that this Southeast Asian country is "still predominantly conservative with leanings toward authoritarianism".

"When will they learn that when they ban or censor a film, the ensuing stink that's raised causes more problems than if the film had been allowed to quietly unspool? Perhaps if people had seen it, they might criticise it, but they'd also talk about the problems in society that allow children to be exploited," he wrote in a blog article entitled 'Children of the Dark Ban Mars Start of Bangkok International Film Festival'.

Given the trafficking of women and children in the region, the producers of *Children of the Dark* thought it was a good way to raise awareness about the issue. Not surprisingly, they were dismayed at the turn of events.

Given the trafficking of women and children in the region, the producers of Children of the Dark *thought it was a good way to raise awareness of the issue.*

In a statement released by the film producers after the ban, the producers expressed their desire to have the film shown in Thailand and the rest of the world. "This film is not just about Thailand. It's about the whole region, helping people on the outside to understand the problem," Japanese producer Masaomi Karasaki was quoted by newspapers as saying.

For MTV Thailand [a Thai music and entertainment channel] campaign director Simon Goff, film as an educational medium can be a very powerful tool, as proven by the widely popular MTV EXIT: End Exploitation and Trafficking documentary launched in 2007. [The] MTV EXIT [documentary] has since been distributed across the region in 12 versions, including Mandarin, Japanese, Korean, Indonesian, Tagalog, Lao, Khmer, Burmese and Vietnamese.

"If you can get a film shown commercially, then it can be a hugely successful way of educating people. Films are very powerful tools and if it's really a good film that shows the issue in its ugly reality and if it's accurate, then I would see no reason why it should be banned just because it's distasteful," Goff said. He cited the award-winning 2006 movie *Blood Diamond* as an example, one that brought to light the plight of those involved in diamond trading.

He declined to comment on the banning of *Children of the Dark* in particular, because he has not seen the movie yet.

ECPAT International (End Child Prostitution, Child Pornography and Trafficking of Children for Sexual Purposes), a nongovernmental organisation working to eliminate the commercial sexual exploitation of children, also abstained from making comments under the circumstances.

"It is very difficult to give a blanket statement as to what is beneficial or not [without having seen the film itself]," stated ECPAT communication officer Caroline Liou.

She, however, reiterated that ECPAT follows strict guidelines when it comes to media coverage involving children.

ECPAT believes that "media can play an important part in promoting children's well-being and respect for their rights by portraying children in a positive way, by seeking children's opinions, and by providing children with avenues for exchanging information and opinions".

Stereotypes, sensationalism, sexualised images of children, to name a few, are no-no's during media coverages, according to ECPAT's media guidelines.

Even Self-Interested Films Should Not Be Censored

Goff clarified that unlike the Japanese-Thai film, theirs is of a different format. "It's not for commercial reasons and we don't aim to sell programming. Ours is educational documentary, not a drama format," he said, adding that the anti-trafficking documentary was given away to Thai authorities, local government organisations and police forces.

Hopefully, he said, MTV's negotiations with Thai PBS to show the documentary to local audiences will pull through soon. "We haven't fallen foul of any issues about censorship and we work with local authorities here and other countries. We play by the book and we haven't had anything censored or banned. We're careful to do it sensitively to ensure that all identities of people in the film are protected and will not adversely affect their lives," said Goff.

Pipope noted that while there are indeed movies that, instead of pushing important issues, are self-serving and merely highlight the skills of the director, censorship still has no place in the industry. "I am all for film ratings and not censorship, and this includes all kinds of films, yes, even the self-serving ones," he said.

"I am all for film ratings and not censorship, and this includes all kinds of films, yes, even the self-serving ones."

"If they (audience) don't like it, they can picket in front of theatres or boycott the film," he added.

Unfortunately, he noted, the Thai public is not as involved as he would like to expect. "Thais, as a whole, don't care because they don't feel it's tampering with their rights. There's not enough public debate going on about this."

According to United Nations [UN] and other studies, human trafficking has a total market value of 32 billion U.S. dollars. More than half of 2.5 million victims of trafficking worldwide are in the Asia-Pacific. At the UN General Assembly for children in August 2007, it was reported that about 1.8 million children became victims of commercial sex trade in 2000. About one million children in Southeast Asia are said to be involved in this trade.

Censorship in Zimbabwe Hinders Local Musicians

Diane Thram

Diane Thram is director of the International Library of African Music and coordinator of the Ethnomusicology Programme at Rhodes University in South Africa. In the following viewpoint, she argues that the political troubles in Zimbabwe have increased music censorship, both official and unofficial. Thram says musicians who agree to support the regime are vilified by the public and lose opportunities for live performances, while those who oppose the regime or remain neutral often cannot get their music distributed or broadcast. Local musicians, Thram concludes, find it almost impossible to have successful musical careers in Zimbabwe.

As you read, consider the following questions:

1. What did Andy Brown do that caused him to lose the respect of his fans, according to Thram?
2. Why does Thram say that Leonard Zhakata called in for questioning by the police in 2004?
3. According to Thram, who are Mapfumo and Mtukudzi, and why do they not need to rely on local airplay?

Diane Thram, "ZVAKWANA!—ENOUGH! Media Control and Unofficial Censorship of Music in Zimbabwe," in *Popular Music Censorship in Africa*, edited by Michael Drewett and Martin Cloonan, Farnham, England: Ashgate Publishing Limited, 2006, pp. 85–87. Copyright © Michael Drewett and Martin Cloonan 2006. All rights reserved. Reproduced by permission.

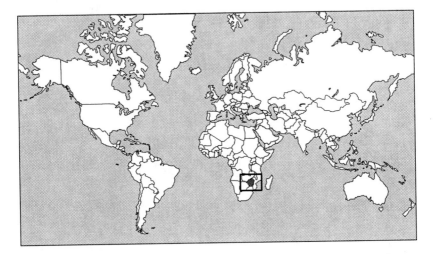

Career damage has been experienced not only by [Zimbabwe] musicians perceived to be anti the [President Robert] Mugabe regime, but also by those with previously successful local careers who have chosen to cooperate with Information Minister [Jonathan] Moyo. It is possible that those who worked for the minister by writing and performing songs for his media campaigns and playing at the regime-sponsored live 'galas' [concerts sponsored by the government] did so because they agree with the regime's political tactics and are truly ultra-patriotic; but there is no doubt that they did so because they need the income from playing at the galas, wanted support to make recordings, and wanted the precious airplay that cooperation with the Information Ministry afforded. However, despite securing airplay, musicians in favour with the regime often lost the respect of their fans and were labeled as 'sellouts'.

Collaboration Damages Artists' Careers

The story of how the government contributed millions of Zimbabwe dollars to set up Andy Brown's Stone Studio has been widely reported. Brown in return adapted, arranged, and produced the music on 'More Fire', one of the Third

Chimurenga[1] series' media campaign recordings. A manager/ event promoter working in Harare [the capital of Zimbabwe] attested to the career damage suffered by Brown in the aftermath and claimed the public has 'demonized' him in reaction to his decision to work for the regime. This manager, who witnessed him being booed by the crowd at a concert, reported that his record sales and opportunities for live performance have both fallen off drastically and that it is generally felt that the damage to his career is irreparable.

Career damage has been experienced not only by musicians perceived to be anti the [President Robert] Mugabe regime, but also by those . . . who have chosen to cooperate with Information Minister [Jonathan] Moyo.

Neutrality Damages Artists' Careers

In contrast there is Leonard Zhakata, a singer/songwriter with great popularity throughout the country ever since he released his first record in 1988. Zhakata claims his lyrics have always spoken to the problems of daily life since long before the onset of the Crisis [the economic and political upheaval in Zimbabwe, beginning around 2000]. However, his career (both in terms of CD sales and income from touring throughout Zimbabwe) has suffered since 2000–2001 when he lost airplay because certain song lyrics in his recent releases have been interpreted as critical of the regime. When Zhakata contacted ZBC radio [Zimbabwe Broadcasting Corporation, the state-controlled radio in Zimbabwe] to ask why his recent recordings are not receiving airplay, ZBC's legal adviser told him that his music has not been banned. Yet when he asked DJs why they no longer play his music, they replied that they were told (they did not say by whom) not to play it because it is 'politically incorrect'. Zhakata says of his music, 'I have fans

1. Chimurenga means a revolutionary struggle, the "Third Chimurenga" refers to land reforms undertaken since 2000 by Mugabe's regime.

from both political parties. I sing a straightforward message meant to be encouragement for everyone. My most popular songs are against exploitation of the weak. I can't abandon that'.

Despite Zhakata's intention to remain politically neutral, in April 2004 the pressure group *Zvakwana* pirated one of his songs for a compilation CD of 'resistance music' they made available for free download from the Internet. When news of the CD got out, the *Standard* [a Zimbabwe newspaper] reported that Zhakata had been called in for questioning by the police. According to Zhakata, the police did not harass him; they were only interested in what he knew about *Zvakwana*, which was nothing. Unfortunately, *Zvakwana* never approached Zhakata for permission to use his song, and by pirating it they further politicized his music, which served to entrench his reputation as an artist who speaks out against the regime, when in fact he views his music as apolitical. Zhakata described the career damage he has suffered by losing airplay as very serious by saying, 'In our part of the world people rely on very few sources of information. Without media support your career is in trouble'.

'In our part of the world people rely on very few sources of information. Without media support your career is in trouble'.

A Climate of Fear

The examples discussed in this [viewpoint] have been presented to support my argument that unofficial/*de facto* censorship of popular music, restriction of free expression, and career damage to pop musicians have become the status quo in Zimbabwe since passage of the Broadcasting Services Act in 2001. Although no 'official' censorship of music by the ZCB [Zimbabwean Censorship Board] has as yet occurred, an album of protest music released by an outspoken Harare pres-

Death Statistics in Zimbabwe, 1970–2008

As the political and economic crisis in Zimbabwe has worsened since 2000, death statistics have also worsened.

	1970	1990	2008
Deaths per 1000 people	13	9	16
Life expectancy (years)	55	61	44

TAKEN FROM: "Zimbabwe-Statistics," *UNICEF*, n.d. www.unicef.org. http://www.unicef.org/infobycountry/zimbabwe_statistics.html.

sure group, the National Constitutional Assembly (NCA) in the aftermath of the 2005 parliamentary election may provide a test case. The NCA album was banned by the police just before its scheduled release at a public event. After the cancellation of the event due to the police ban, the NCA decided to release the album on 18 May 2005 in defiance of the police ban, arguing that the police had no authority to ban it. In response the regime sent the album to the ZCB for assessment. The ZCB's decision in this case has not been reported to date, perhaps because news of the regime's *Murambatsvina* clean-up campaign [known as Operation Murambatsvina, in which the regime began forcibly clearing slums, displacing millions]— instigated the following day—has dominated the press ever since.

The information presented in this [viewpoint] gives a glimpse of on-the-ground realities during the time of my field research and as such speaks only for the conditions and opinions of those interviewed during that particular historical moment. From it I have drawn the following conclusion: The ruling party's resurrection of the cultural nationalism of the Second Chimurenga [Zimbabwe's war of independence 1964–79] with its Third Chimurenga series' media campaigns, together with the ultra-patriotic themes of the government-sponsored 'galas' has set musicians up to be used by the regime to promote its ideology through the music they are commissioned to write and perform. Musicians who prefer to be apolitical and those who refuse to work for the regime on moral grounds face the threat of no work and no airplay, plus the fear of more serious repercussions if their music is viewed as critical of ruling-party policies. The regime's isolationist rhetoric of patriotism and sovereignty that was written into the song lyrics on the Information Minister's CD/cassette releases deliberately created an enemy in the menacing Western 'other' which contributed to the climate of fear prevalent throughout the country.

Musicians who prefer to be apolitical and those who refuse to work for the regime on moral grounds face the threat of no work and no airplay, plus the fear of more serious repercussions.

I further conclude that the impact of the Broadcasting Services Act's legislated media control and the attendant restriction of free expression actualized by the Ministry of Information under Jonathan Moyo's leadership has been felt most acutely by musicians with local careers who, as creative artists, feel a need to honestly express themselves through their music. These are the many musicians who, unlike the Zimbabwean superstars [Thomas] Mapfumo and [Oliver] Mtukudzi, have not established global recognition and therefore rely on local airplay and live performance opportunities to establish their careers. They do not have the luxury of recording contracts and international distributors for their recordings. It quickly becomes apparent that issues of power and powerlessness are paramount in a reality that finds musicians, when they express the truth of their experience in their song lyrics, with no access to airplay. Without airplay and with very few venues for live performance beyond the ruling party–sponsored 'galas', there is little chance for a musician in Zimbabwe who performs popular music to mount a successful career.

In the United States, Viewing Manga Depicting Child Pornography Should Not Be Illegal

Lawrence A. Stanley

Lawrence A. Stanley is a lawyer specializing in trademark and copyright law. His articles have been published in Playboy, *the* Washington Post, *the* Gauntlet *and other print publications. In the following viewpoint, he discusses the case of Christopher Handley, who was arrested and prosecuted for owning manga (Japanese comics) drawings depicting sexualized images of minors. Stanley argues that drawings in which no children were actually harmed cannot be treated as child pornography. Stanley concludes that the prosecution of Handley was unconstitutional and that it will damage First Amendment rights.*

As you read, consider the following questions:

1. According to Stanley, what did the search of Handley's home turn up, and what did it not turn up?
2. Before 1984, what was forbidden under U.S. child pornography laws, according to Stanley?
3. What does Stanley say may be criminalized by the case of *United States v. Schales*?

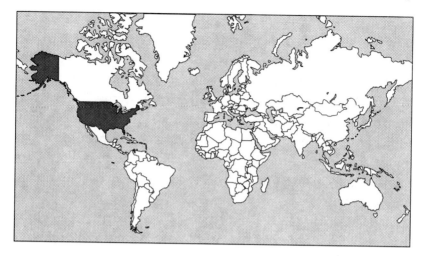

Paragraph (a)(1) of Section 1466A of the U.S. Criminal Code criminalizes the production, distribution, receipt and possession with intent to distribute of any obscene visual depiction, including a drawing, cartoon, sculpture, or painting, which "depicts a minor engaging in sexually explicit conduct." Section(b)(1) purports to criminalize the private possession of such representations. "Minor" means any person under the age of eighteen and "sexually explicit conduct" is defined as in the child pornography statute: "actual or *simulated*" acts of sexual intercourse, oral and anal sex, bestiality, masturbation, "sadistic or masochistic abuse," or "lascivious exhibition of the genitals or pubic area of any person."

Child Pornography Is Not the Same as Obscenity

Despite the application of both child pornography definitions and sentencing standards to Section 1466a, obscenity is not the same thing as child pornography. An item is child pornography only when it depicts an actual minor engaged in sexually explicit conduct, regardless of the conditions under [which] it is made, the quality or character of its portrayal or the mores of the community in which it is found. (For this reason "virtual child pornography" is not child pornography at all under the law. It is an oxymoron.) By contrast, an item is obscene when a jury finds it so after applying the three-pronged test devised in 1973 by the Supreme Court in the case of *Miller v. California*. To be clear, "obscenity" is not synonymous with pornography, but a tiny subcategory of it, which, in one jurisdiction or another, is found by a jury (or a judge acting in a jury's stead) to be illegal. Nothing, not even pornography, is presumptively "obscene." It must be judged so in a court of law. . . .

On March 6, 2006, a jury found [Dwight] Whorley guilty for "receiving" obscene cartoons. It also found him guilty for receiving child pornography photos of naked minors and obscene e-mails. However, for the cartoons alone he was sentenced to 20 years in prison, with a 10-year period of probation thereafter, a sentence which was upheld on appeal last December [2008] by the 4th Circuit Court of Appeals. Had he not been previously convicted of receiving child pornography, his sentence would probably have been much lower, but under 1466A the sentence for the first-time receipt of even a single image is, in any event, "not less than 5 years and not more than 20 years."

An item is child pornography only when it depicts an actual minor engaged in sexually explicit conduct.

Cartoons Are Not Child Pornography

Given all the qualifying facts in the *Whorley* case, one might ask, why should anyone care? Setting aside questions of fundamental justice for the moment, the answer is: because cartoons and drawings aren't child pornography and should not be treated as such under the law. The moral slippage in the law is palpable in the way it conflates images of actual minors with fictional representations: It refers to "depictions of minors," and, by reference to the other provisions in the law, defines acts engaged in by "persons," but how is a cartoon character a person? It talks about engaging in sexually explicit acts, but how does a cartoon character engage in anything? It defines "actual or simulated" conduct, but how can a cartoon character's conduct be "actual"? Ultimately the law denies the reality that these are not "depictions of minors" at all but pure fantasy. One should care about this case because *United States v. Whorley* was a testing of the waters. With Whorley behind bars, some people in the government believe they have a mandate.

Christopher Handley's circumstances were vastly different from Dwight Whorley's when law enforcement officers followed him home from the Post Office on May 23, 2006. He had just picked up a package from Japan containing manga [Japanese comics]. A thorough search of his home turned up only more of it: some 1200 magazines, hundreds of DVDs, laser discs and videotapes, and an untold number of images on computer, but no child pornography or even images of nude minors. Handley was a collector of manga, not *lolicon* [a genre of manga that includes sexualized images of young girls], and the vast majority of the manga and images he possessed contained no fantasy representations of minors at all. The fact that a small amount of it represented fictional prepubescents and fantasy portrayals of sadomasochistic or violent sex, however, meant that Handley faced a sentence ranging from a minimum of 7 years and 3 months in prison to a maximum of 9 years.

What does a small amount mean? By the government's count, he received or possessed more than 150 but less than 300 such images in total. Not 150 to 300 magazines, but cartoon pages with one or more panels or individual jpgs. . . .

Expanding Censorship

How far will the government go? . . . Once you begin to attack pure fantasy, where do you stop? Under current legal interpretation, a drawing of Rin's [a manga and anime character] fictional panties covering her non-existent genitalia constitutes a prohibited sexual act. . . .

Cartoons and drawings are not child pornography and should not be treated as such under the law.

The government, of course, says "trust us," but history teaches precisely the opposite. Since 1984, the category of material that could and would be prosecuted has been in a constant state of expansion by act of Congress and court decision alike. At first the law forbade only the commercial handling of obscene images depicting minors under sixteen. In 1984 the upper age limit was increased to eighteen and the crime of simple receipt was added. Later, Congress included the crime of possession of three or more items, then just a single item. Rather than defining "lascivious exhibitions of the genitals" by the model's pose, the courts interpreted the phrase broadly, basing the determination on factors outside of the image itself, such as whether it was published with a lewd caption or created with lewd intentions in mind. With *United States v. Knox* the meaning of the phrase expanded to include "exhibitions" of the pubic area or genitals that were fully covered by clothing and/or zooming in on that body part from afar, even without the knowledge of the person depicted. Simulated sexual acts were also defined and prohibited. Advertisements became illegal, as did, briefly, any image that "appeared to be" a minor. Then Section 1466A came along, and with it all the criteria and penalties associated with child pornography were applied to completely fictional representations. Naturally the penalties increased with each amendment. Soon, if the so-called "Safety Act," currently [2009] pending before Congress, is passed, the sentence for receiving even a single prohibited cartoon in violation of Section 1466A will jump from "not less than 5 years and not more than 20 years" to "15 years or for life." Life. For cartoons.

Christopher Handley Pleads Guilty

Christopher Handley, 39, of Glenwood, Iowa, pleaded guilty today [May 20, 2009] in Des Moines, Iowa, to possessing obscene visual representations of the sexual abuse of children and mailing obscene material.

According to court documents, in May 2006, U.S. Immigration and Customs Enforcement (ICE) intercepted a mail package coming into the United States from Japan that was addressed to Handley. Inside the package was obscene material, including books containing visual representations of the sexual abuse of children, specifically Japanese *manga* drawings of minor females being sexually abused by adult males and animals. Pursuant to a search warrant, the U.S. Postal Inspection Service searched and seized additional obscene drawings of the sexual abuse of children at Handley's residence in Glenwood. . . .

Pursuant to his plea agreement, Handley today pleaded guilty to one count of possessing obscene visual representations of the sexual abuse of children in violation of Title 18, United States [Criminal] Code, Section 1466A(b)(1), which prohibits the possession of any type of visual depiction . . . that depicts a minor engaging in sexually explicit conduct that is obscene.

Handley also agreed to plead guilty to one count of mailing obscene material and to forfeit all seized property. Handley faces a maximum of 15 years in prison, a maximum fine of $250,000, and a three-year term of supervised release.

U.S. Department of Justice Office of Public Affairs,
"Iowa Man Pleads Guilty to Possessing Obscene
Visual Representations of the Sexual Abuse of Children,"
May 20, 2009. www.justice.gov.

Thought Control

Artists probably have the most to fear. Under *United States v. Schales*, a decision issued last October [2008] by the Ninth Circuit Court of Appeals, the very act of drawing may be deemed criminal under Section 1466A. In that case the defendant was charged and convicted for "producing" obscenity by using software to edit and paste together parts of preexisting pornography with legal photos he took of local girls to make it appear as if the girls were engaging in sexually explicit conduct. (He did not disseminate these images, but kept them for his private viewing.) There is no logical reason why one rule would apply to collages and another to drawings and paintings. Following this decision, what artist is willing to risk an assessment of the worth of his or her work by the harshest critic of all, the criminal law?

The government of course says "trust us," but history teaches precisely the opposite.

It is often said that "bad cases make bad law," but here the bad law is being made by legislators and judges alike who climb over each other in an effort to prove their moral uprightness and supposed concern with protecting children. It is quite possible that at least some of the more obvious excesses—the prosecution of private possession of obscenity; the definition of "production" to include the creation of collages; the definition of "receiving" to include viewing online however briefly (or not at all); and the recent criminalization of "accessing" with intent to view—will eventually be ruled unconstitutional. Likewise, there are solid legal arguments why the interpretation of Section 1466A as applying to completely fictional representations is untenable and contradictory given both the language of the statute and statements of intent by those in Congress who drafted it. But in the broader view, Section 1466A is about thought control. Both the law and its penalties are premised solely on the idea that fictional representations "whet the appetites" of sex offenders or seduce children into sex. When the Supreme Court rejected that rationale for prohibiting fictional representations under the rubric of "child pornography" but held that such images could, nonetheless, be prohibited if they were "obscene," it did not indicate that anything goes. Rather, the Court announced this crucial principle:

> The mere tendency of speech to encourage unlawful acts is not a sufficient reason for banning it. The government "cannot constitutionally premise legislation on the desirability of controlling a person's private thoughts." . . . First Amendment freedoms are most in danger when the government seeks to control thought or to justify its laws for that impermissible end. The right to think is the beginning of freedom, and speech must be protected from the government because speech is the beginning of thought.

In the broader view, Section 1466A is about thought control.

Speech includes not just the written word, but also painting, drawing, collage, film, video and sculpture. Private authorship and possession of obscene *books* are no different from private authorship or possession of obscene *works of art*. Prohibiting either strikes at the very heart of freedom of thought, but then so does prohibiting an individual's right to buy, purchase, download or otherwise receive "obscenity" for his or her private consumption. Don't think that this argument is a defense of child pornography. It isn't. The subject here is fiction and fantasy. No children are abused in the production of these images.

Jamaican Dancehall Performers Who Espouse Homophobia Should Be Prevented from Performing in Canada

Krishna Rau

Krishna Rau writes for Xtra, a Canadian Web site devoted to homosexual issues. In the following viewpoint, he notes that many Jamaican dancehall performers sing songs that encourage hatred of and violence against homosexuals. Rau interviews experts and activists who suggest that it is reasonable to prevent these performers from appearing in Canada.

As you read, consider the following questions:

1. Concerts by which performers were canceled, according to Krishna Rau?

2. What kind of violence against gays did the Jamaica Forum for Lesbians, All-Sexuals and Gays report as occurring in 2005, 2006, and the early part of 2007?

3. How does Rinaldo Walcott believe dancehall has affected attitudes toward gays and lesbians as it has spread to countries throughout the Caribbean?

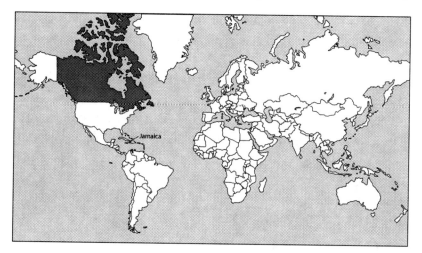

As it did in October [2007] a coalition of queer, black and human rights groups has succeeded in preventing Jamaican musicians from performing in Canada.

Violating Hate Crime Laws

Shows by dancehall [a genre of Jamaican popular music] musicians Capleton, Baby Cham and Beenie Man have all been cancelled. The artists were scheduled to perform in southern Ontario in November and December [2007]. The Stop Murder Music (Canada) coalition (SMM) opposed their entry into the country on the grounds of homophobic lyrics the coalition says violate Canada's hate laws.

The Stop Murder Music (Canada) coalition (SMM) opposed their entry into the country on the grounds of homophobic lyrics the coalition says violate Canada's hate laws.

"All three are gone," says Helen Kennedy, the executive director of queer lobby group Egale Canada, a member of SMM. "None of the artists who violate our criminal code will perform, which is good news. Our objective is to raise the awareness of the human rights violations when these artists come to this country."

Kennedy says SMM sent a letter to Minister of [Citizenship and] Immigration Diane Finley asking her to deny entry to the artists on the grounds that their songs violate Canada's hate laws. But Kennedy says they have received no reply. Nobody from Finley's office returned calls from Xtra [a Canadian Web site].

Jamaican Homophobia

SMM met with the promoters of the Baby Cham and Beenie Man shows and demanded the artists publicly sign—in Jamaica—the Reggae Compassionate Act, a contract in which the artist apologizes for writing and performing homophobic songs and pledges not to perform them any more.

Kennedy says she thinks the artists probably didn't take well to the demand.

"One can guess that the conversation didn't go very well," she says.

The promoters did not return phone calls or e-mails from Xtra.

According to Akim Larcher, the founder of the Canadian chapter of SMM, artists have in the past signed such a declaration before shows in North America or Europe then repudiated it when home in Jamaica.

Attacks on queers in Jamaica are widespread.

"The most important thing would be a public apology within the Caribbean, especially in Jamaica, specifically saying violence against gays and lesbians is not acceptable and should not be tolerated," says Larcher.

According to Amnesty International and gay human rights groups, attacks on queers in Jamaica are widespread. The Jamaica Forum for Lesbians, All-Sexuals and Gays reports that 98 queers were attacked this year [2007] between February and July in 43 mob attacks and that at least 10 queers were murdered between 2005 and 2006.

According to SMM, Capleton, who was scheduled to perform on Nov 24 in Woodbridge, has songs like "Give Har" which includes the lyrics "Shoulda know seh Capleton bun battyman [You should know that Capleton burns queers]/ Dem same fire apply to all di lesbian [The same fire applies to lesbians]/ Seh mi bun everything from mi know seh dem gay [Say I burn everything as long as I know that they're gay]/ All boogaman and sodemites fi get killed [All queers and sodomites should be killed]."

Beenie Man, who was to perform in Waterloo on Dec 7, performs "Han Up Deh" with the lyrics "Hang chi chi gal wid a long piece of rope [Hang lesbians with a long piece of rope]" and "Batty Man Fi Dead" which means "Queers must be killed." . . .

Baby Cham, who was going to perform at Toronto's Sound Academy on Dec 8 as part of the Jingle Jam event, is credited with "Bun Batty Bwoy [Burn gay men]" and "Another Level" with the lyrics "Poop man fi drawn and dat a yawd man philosophy [Shit men must be drowned and that's a Jamaican philosophy]."

In an interview before the news of Baby Cham's cancellation Carey Britt, the director of marketing at Sound Academy, says he wasn't aware that Baby Cham was scheduled to perform. He says that because of the controversy, the promoters may have been trying to downplay the musician's presence.

"They may be trying to pull a sneaky one," he says. "We've got it listed in the calendar as Jingle Jam, not a concert."

Britt says that when Croatian artist Thompson—who has been accused of glorifying Nazis—was prevented from performing at Kool Haus in November for his alleged fascist sympathies, the promoters merely told Sound Academy they needed a bigger venue. Sound Academy cancelled that show.

Kennedy says SMM met with several Jamaican and black community groups on Nov 13 to discuss music with hateful lyrics and other issues affecting both communities. She says the groups will meet again.

Larcher says that since SMM gained a great deal of publicity in October when artists Elephant Man and Sizzla had several shows cancelled the Jamaican community in Canada has been discussing the issue.

"It's been positive and negative from the Jamaican-Canadian community," he says. "There is still that underlying issue of homophobia."

Larcher says that some in the black gay community have accused SMM of targeting Jamaica.

"In no way do we demean Jamaica," he says. "But it's the epicentre of where that music comes from and the epicentre of violence against gays and lesbians."

Music Could Cause Harm

Academic and author Rinaldo Walcott—who teaches and writes about black popular culture—says it is the dancehall artists who are demeaning Jamaica. He says he has no patience for arguments that the homophobic songs reflect Jamaican culture.

"Anyone who makes that argument is saying Jamaica is a deeply ingrained homophobic culture and that's a bullshit argument," says Walcott. "This music is not a useful reflection of the complexity of the culture of black people.

"This would be like 10 or 15 rock bands in Canada making hateful music about gays and people saying, 'That's just what Canada's like.'"

But Walcott says that as queers in the Caribbean have begun to speak up, music has become a source of opposition.

Violence Against Homosexuals in Jamaica

Violent acts against men who have sex with men are commonplace in Jamaica. Verbal and physical violence, ranging from beatings to brutal armed attacks to murder, are widespread. . . . Men who have sex with men and women who have sex with women reported being driven from their homes and their towns by neighbors who threatened to kill them if they remained, forcing them to abandon their possessions and leaving many homeless.

Human Rights Watch, "Hated to Death:
Homophobia, Violence, and Jamaica's HIV/AIDS Epidemic,"
November 15, 2004. www.hrw.org.

"As gays and lesbians have organized the music has become one of the main vehicles to respond," he says. "There's also a lot of anecdotal evidence that as dancehall spreads to other Caribbean countries, we've also seen a change in the tone of the homophobia. It used to be laughter and ridicule. Now it's verging on and sometimes turning to violence."

Walcott says that while he doesn't think the music will lead to violence in Canada, it could affect queer blacks, especially youth.

Walcott says that while he doesn't think the music will lead to violence in Canada, it could affect queer blacks, especially youth.

"It could hurt someone who might be struggling to come out. It could make the lives of black gays and lesbians more difficult and less meaningful."

Walcott says that he also doesn't think the issue is one of censorship.

"This music represents hate to such an extreme that it calls for the extermination of gays and lesbians. Stop Murder Music is not about censorship. It's saying that certain kinds of speech that are so hateful are not welcome in our society and under our legal system."

National Socialist Black Metal Should Not Be Sold Through Mainstream Outlets

Simon Cressy

Simon Cressy writes for Searchlight, *a British antiracist and antifascist magazine. In the following viewpoint, he argues that National Socialist black metal (NSBM) deliberately espouses white supremacy, anti-Semitism, and violence. Nonetheless, Cressy notes, music by these groups, and by other extreme black metal bands with NSBM sympathies, is distributed through mainstream outlets, especially in the United Kingdom. Cressy concludes that mainstream companies should cease selling the music.*

As you read, consider the following questions:

1. According to Cressy, why did the National Alliance (NA) take over Cymophane?
2. From what country do Drudkh, Hate Forest, and Dark Ages come, and what beliefs does Cressy say they espouse?
3. How does Cressy define ZOG?

Varg Vikernes's conviction for murder in 1993 was a baptism of fire for National Socialist black metal [NSBM, a type of music that explicitly promotes Nazism and fascism].

Although the Norwegian remains in prison, 15 years on NSBM has become big business and is being sold online by household name companies.

Varg Vikernes is the poster boy for the National Socialist black metal genre. Under the name "Count Grishnackh" he secured his place in black metal history after murdering Øystein Aarseth, who played with the black metal band Mayhem.

An Icon for NSBM

Aarseth, also known as Euronymous, was found dead outside his apartment in Oslo with 23 stab wounds, two to the head, five to the neck and 16 to the back. The motive for the murder is believed to have been a power struggle between Vikernes and Aarseth and disagreements over finances within the black metal scene.

Vikernes, 35, was sentenced to 21 years in prison. The Norwegian Ministry of Justice has just turned down his latest request for parole [2008], on the grounds that he was "too dangerous" to be released.

As well as the murder Vikernes, who was then a Satanist but has since renounced his beliefs and embraced Norse gods and Nazism instead, was found guilty of several arsons and attempted arsons of churches. He also admitted planning to blow up the Blitz House, a leftist centre in Oslo.

As well as the murder Vikernes ... was found guilty of several arsons and attempted arsons of churches.

Despite the seriousness of his crimes, after he had served less than half his sentence, he was transferred to a minimum security prison in Tonsberg to prepare for his release. But in 2003 he failed to return after being given 17 hours' leave of absence.

He was soon recaptured in a stolen car and in possession of a Heckler & Koch AG-3 assault rifle, a handgun, numerous large knives, a gas mask, camouflage clothing, a laptop, a compass, a global positioning system, various maps and a fake passport. It emerged that the rifle had been stolen from an armoury 14 years earlier.

For his escape attempt, which included hijacking a car at gunpoint, a mere 13 months were added to his sentence.

Although Vikernes's lyrics are not Nazi, since his conviction he and his band, Burzum, of which he is the only member, have become icons for both NSBM and black metal as a whole.

Growing Profits from NSBM

Burzum and NSBM have also become highly profitable. In July 2000, the Chicago-based Center for New Community discovered that William Pierce, founder and leader of the white nationalist National Alliance (NA) and owner of Resistance Records, had gained control of Cymophane Records, an NSBM specialist label in which Vikernes had been involved.

Pierce, who died in 2002, was the author of *The Turner Diaries*, the futuristic race-war fantasy novel that inspired Timothy McVeigh to detonate a truck full of explosives in front of the Alfred P. Murrah Federal Building in Oklahoma City in 1995, killing 167 people.

The main purpose of the NA's takeover of Cymophane was to gain the rights to distribute Burzum albums in the USA. The NA also set up Unholy Records as a subsidiary of Resistance Records to distribute the 2002 compilation album, *Visions—A Tribute to Burzum*, internationally after the Center for New Community blocked attempts to get it distributed by the Dutch East India Trading Company.

Unholy is managed by Ymir G Winter, who plays guitar in Grom, a New York-based NSBM band. Winter told the US heavy metal magazine *Decibel* in 2007 that his father openly advocated fascism and that his grandfather fought for Germany in the Second World War.

"During many of our shows, we will spit fire and then set an Israeli flag ablaze," Winter went on. "When regulations don't allow this, we have the crowd stomp the Israeli flag and spit on it."

Winter, an NA member, is responsible for recruiting bands for Resistance Records and writes for the label's magazine *Resistance*. "Resistance wants to promote Aryan awareness and does so by using music as a recruitment tool and as a vessel for the National Socialist/White Power movement," continued Winter.

Resistance Records seems to have found it easier to distribute the Burzum tribute CD in the UK [United Kingdom] than in the US [United States]. A quick surf online revealed HMV, Amazon UK and Play.com among those selling the NSBM CD.

Resistance Records seems to have found it easier to distribute the Burzum tribute CD in the UK than in the US.

Searchlight made several attempts to obtain a comment from HMV [an entertainment retail chain] and eventually reached Gennaro Castaldo, the company's head of press and public relations. In response to his request for more information we sent him a very detailed e-mail outlining the history of Resistance Records and its links to the NA.

However he was unable to offer any explanation as to why a white supremacist organisation was able to peddle its wares through HMV. After a long delay Castaldo replied: "I regret that I can only say that I am not in a position to make an informed comment at this time. I apologise for any inconvenience this may cause you."

It is unclear what information Castaldo needs to make "an informed comment" but we will publish whatever we receive in a future issue of *Searchlight*.

Extreme Black Metal

HMV, Amazon [UK] and Play.com also carry a large amount of stock from Supernal Music, a label that is also the biggest online distributor of "extreme black metal".

Supernal bands such as Drudkh, Hate Forest and Dark Ages, all from Ukraine, are considered fairly mainstream within the NSBM genre. Their CDs are widely available via most of the online music stores. These bands are not blatant about their far right, racist and anti-Semitic views but mask them in pseudo-intellectual and romantic ancestor worship nationalism. Visit the Supernal Web site, however, and a whole host of racist and offensive CDs are available.

These bands are not blatant about their far right, racist and anti-Semitic views but mask them in pseudo-intellectual and romantic ancestor worship nationalism.

Based in Cranleigh, Surrey, Supernal has been run by its owner Alex Kurtagic since 1996. Kurtagic is also a recording artist with the odd sounding group Benighted Leams.

His monthly bulletin to Supernal subscribers has caused some alarm among his customers. Front cover pictures of musicians have gradually been replaced by historical figures admired by the far right, including Savitri Devi the Nazi mystic and writer, the anti-Semitic writer Ernst Jünger, the Chilean Nazi Miguel Serrano and Julius Langbehn, a 19th century anti-Semite.

Supernal's catalogue reveals its true agenda. One CD is by the US group Sturmführer entitled *Ich Kämpfe* (I fight). Track one, "Treu Martyr," includes a speech by Robert Mathews, leader of the US Nazi terrorist group The Order, whom the song depicts as a hero and martyr.

Another Supernal CD is the Capricornus/Der Stürmer split album titled *Polish-Hellenic Alliance Against ZOG*. ZOG stands for Zionist Occupation Government, an anti-Semitic conspiracy theory according to which Jews control government. Der Stürmer is a Greek band closely linked to the Greek section of the Nazi bonehead outfit Blood & Honour and the Nazi group Golden Dawn.

Included on the CD is a song called "The Nailbomber," which is a tribute to David Copeland, the British Nazi bomber and former BNP [British National Party, a far-right political party] member [who set a series of bombs in April 1999 that killed three and injured 129]. Included with the track are original recordings from police interviews with Copeland after his arrest.

Der Stürmer also contributed to a compilation CD that raised money for German Nazi prisoners including Erich Priebke, convicted in 1996 for war crimes for his part in the SS [an organ of the Nazi Party] massacre of 335 Italian civilians at the Ardeatine caves in Rome in 1944.

Other bands carried by Supernal include Kiborg and Vandal from Russia, both of which are closely linked with Russian Blood & Honour. Another is Xenophobia from the US, whose singer Brian Mouldry, aka Warhead Jewgrinder, is linked to the white supremacist Creativity Movement, formerly the [World] Church of the Creator.

NSBM has succeeded in penetrating the online lists of household name businesses and thence teenagers' bedrooms at an alarming rate. It is already on the fringes of the mainstream. Responsible companies such as HMV need to push it back into the gutter where it rightfully belongs.

Periodical Bibliography

The following articles have been selected to supplement the diverse views presented in this chapter.

Article 19: Global Campaign for Free Expression	"Unveiled: Art and Censorship in Iran," September 2006. www.article19.org.
BBC News	"Iran's Underground Music Challenge," May 8, 2006. http://news.bbc.co.uk.
Clifford Coonan	"Censors Lay Down the Law in China," *Independent*, March 16, 2008. www.independent.co.uk.
France 24	"Censorship—Live on Russian TV," September 9, 2008. http://observers.france24.com.
Tim Franks	"Jerusalem Diary: 16 March," BBC News, March 16, 2009. http://news.bbc.co.uk.
GamePolitics.com	"Venezuela: Violent Games Banned, Internet Censorship Next?" March 15, 2010. www.gamepolitics.com.
GroundReport.com	"Banned and Censored Singer Launches Own News Site," March 23, 2010. www.groundreport.com.
Roland Kelts	"Manga, Anime and Trans-cultural Censorship," *Comics Journal*, March 23, 2010. www.tcj.com.
Southern Poverty Law Center	"Darker Than Black," Fall 2000. www.splcenter.org.

CHAPTER 4

Popular Culture's Impact on Attitudes

American Television Shows Undermine Christian Beliefs

Robert Velarde

Robert Velarde is author of a number of books, including Conversations with C.S. Lewis: Imaginative Discussions About Life, Christianity and God. *In the following viewpoint, he argues that television shows* 24 *and* Lost *support utilitarianism and ethical egoism, both of which are opposed to Christianity. Utilitarianism determines right or wrong on the basis of what is good for the greatest number of people, while egoism believes that one should do what is best for oneself. Christians, however, are supposed to do what is right on the basis of moral absolutes and God's word, says Velarde. Velarde suggests, therefore, that it is important for Christians who watch these shows to evaluate them carefully.*

As you read, consider the following questions:

1. Why does Velarde say we should seek to understand the ethical theories promoted on television?

2. According to Velarde, why does ethical egoism break down?

3. Utilitarianism has no foundation for what, according to Velarde?

Robert Velarde, "The Lost Ethics of Pop Culture," Focus on the Family, 2007. Used with permission.

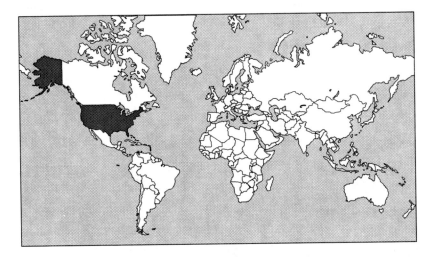

Jack Bauer is in a tough situation. If he doesn't act quickly, thousands of innocent people will die. With little time to sort through the implications of his actions, Jack decides that the best thing to do is torture someone. It seems the most expedient way to provide the greatest good to the greatest number. Such is life every Monday night on Fox's intense drama, *24.*

Meanwhile, on another television network—ABC—the survivors of a downed commercial airliner find themselves on a tropical island full of intrigue and danger. The program, *Lost,* features a con man named Sawyer who often does what needs to be done out of self-interest, a sentiment that is echoed in his words, "every man for himself."

Utilitarianism

Popular culture sometimes mirrors the sentiments of culture in general. Both *24* and *Lost* are no exceptions. In the examples above, *24* presents a particular theory of ethics, while *Lost* presents another. While many watch television uncritically, simply for entertainment value, it is important to understand the underpinnings of entertainment when it comes to worldview questions such as ethics.

As a branch of philosophy addressing questions of right and wrong, ethics plays a crucial and regular role in our lives. By seeking to understand the ethical theories promoted on television and in other forms of popular culture, we can gain better insights into our own ethical systems and determine whether or not they can hold up under real-life conditions.

While many watch television uncritically . . . it is important to understand the underpinnings of entertainment when it comes to worldview questions such as ethics.

Utilitarianism is exemplified in the opening words of this [viewpoint] through the actions of Jack Bauer. It seems that just about every other week Jack has to torture someone in order to save the day. Utilitarianism seeks to determine right or wrong on the basis of whether it is harmful or beneficial to the greatest number of people. A particular act is not viewed as inherently right or wrong. Instead, the focus is the outcome.

According to J.P. Moreland and William Craig [in the book *Philosophical Foundations for a Christian Worldview*], "The essence of utilitarianism can be stated in this way: *the rightness or wrongness of an act or moral rule is solely a matter of the non-moral good produced directly or individually in the consequences of that act or rule.*"

An act utilitarian is not concerned with moral rules, but instead seeks to follow general guidelines that are apparently present in society and have stood the test of time. A rule utilitarian, however, believes that if a generally accepted rule has been deemed good, such a rule should not be violated.

Utilitarianism has several shortcomings. Who decides what is beneficial or harmful to the most people in the long term? On what basis is something deemed "beneficial" or "harmful"? Based on our limited understanding, it is conceivable to choose what may appear to be the greatest good at a particular time, but what of the future? A utilitarian decision may seem justified at the time, only to end up causing problems in the future. Utilitarianism may also be used to justify immoral actions such as slavery. After all, according to the principles of utilitarianism, the enslavement of a minority is a small price to pay for the benefit of a majority.

Egoism and Relativism

The focus of ethical egoism is self-interest, exemplified most consistently in *Lost* by the character Sawyer, noted above. For ethical egoists, the best ethical decision in a given situation must be decided based on the positive and/or negative outcomes as they apply to the self.

Those who adhere to ethical egoism seek solutions to moral dilemmas on the basis of the amount of good or bad that will result from a decision. The ideal is to make an ethical decision that results in the greatest long-term good for the self.

Ethical egoism breaks down because it offers no suitable means of settling ethical disputes. What happens when egos with opposite self-interests collide? What source can be called upon to settle conflict? Without appealing to guidance from another worldview or ethical system, egoism cannot survive as a self-contained ethical system. At some point it must appeal to some other source or authority to settle disagreements. And what if everyone at all times lived as an ethical egoist? Could such a society based solely on self-interest survive? As ethicist Scott Rae observes [in the book *Moral Choices: An Introduction to Ethics*], "ethical egoism ultimately collapses into anarchy."

Ethical relativists reject absolute standards of morality that apply to all people at all times in all cultures. Instead, ethical relativism is subjective. Morality, then, is variable depending on an individual or culture. Cultural relativism asserts that

---

Christian Concerns About Television

In the Beatitudes Jesus said, "They are blessed whose thoughts are pure, for they will see God" (Matthew 5:8). The pervasive worldliness of television can gradually smudge our spiritual sight, the way eyeglasses pick up dust and smudges unnoticed by the person wearing them. While nothing we watch may be terrible, all that inane comedy, green-eyed commercials, gruesome cop shows, or earth-bound love stories can smudge our view of God until we can no longer pray in faith (if we pray at all), nor worship adoringly, nor serve wholeheartedly; all because we no longer see God clearly.

Christianity Today International,
Faith and Pop Culture: Christianity Today Study Series.
Nashville, TN: Thomas Nelson, 2009, p. 66.

---

cultures manufacture their own values and, consequently, they are not based on objective standards.

There are many problems with ethical relativism. First, it does not logically allow for the condemnation of behavior generally viewed as wrong, such as genocide. Second, ethical relativism cannot praise what might be termed cultural reformers. To be a cultural reformer is to go against the predominate view of the time, which ethical relativists would say is culturally determined. As a result, people like Mother Teresa or Martin Luther King Jr. would be going against the mandates of cultural relativism even though what they are standing against is clearly wrong. Third, ethical relativism is self-contradictory in that it simultaneously states that absolutes do not exist, but proposes that ethical relativism is presumably absolute.

Christian Ethics

The predominant influence on Christian ethics is found in divine command and virtue ethics. God reveals Himself and His wishes to us via special revelation, such as through the Bible. God is not arbitrary in His commands. Rather, they are rooted in His good nature. The New Testament stresses aspects of virtue ethics, which emphasizes the development of character. Christ often noted the importance of one's internal condition and motivations.

Some Christians also emphasize what is known as natural law. Unlike special revelation, natural law may be found in general revelation, such as in creation or, with regard to ethics, it is something that is inherently known at least to some degree....

Given the significance of our ethical decisions, it's important to understand the ramifications of our behavior and how our choices fit into larger issues.

In contrast to relativism, Christianity believes that moral absolutes are rooted in God's nature. Unlike the self-centeredness of ethical egoism, Christ taught His followers to love God and place Him in a position of supremacy and to love others. While followers of utilitarianism seek the greatest good for the greatest number, the system has no foundation for calling anything "good" or "bad." The Bible calls us to do what is right in God's eyes, not what seems prudent simply because of how we may think it will benefit the most number of people in the long run or how it might benefit ourselves.

Of course, most people don't go through life analyzing all their actions and determining whether or not they fit into a particular ethical system. In many instances, we just react without really thinking through the worldview implications of our moral choices. However, given the significance of our ethical decisions, it's important to understand the ramifications of our behavior and how our choices fit into larger issues.

Shows like *24* and *Lost* communicate ethical messages that everyone should be prepared to evaluate, especially in light of what corresponds to the reality of God's truth when it comes to right and wrong.

Television Does Not Encourage Obesity

Catharine Lumby and Duncan Fine

Catharine Lumby is a columnist for the Sydney Morning Herald *and an associate professor of media studies at the University of Sydney. Duncan Fine is a writer and director specializing in children's media who has written for the shows Hi-5 and Bambaloo, and for programs on Playhouse Disney. In this viewpoint, they argue that television has long been blamed for increasing obesity. However, they say, the evidence linking TV and weight gain is weak. Instead, they conclude, obesity is linked to socioeconomic and other cultural factors that have little to do with television.*

As you read, consider the following questions:

1. Who do the authors say are the heaviest viewers of television?
2. According to Mike Stratton's study, what was the most reliable indicator for whether a child did not play sports?
3. The U.S. Centers for Disease Control and Prevention found that obesity in children is much higher among which groups?

What could be more lazy, more self-indulgent, more stupid than a fat person watching TV? You can picture the scene—an unkempt living room covered in pizza boxes and Coke cans, three-day growth, four-day-old underpants, a down-at-heel sofa and a 24-hour Jerry Springer [Jerry Springer hosted a talk show that was widely considered to be trashy] marathon. Now think again. Would it change things if we tidied up the room, put in a plasma screen Sony TV, a gourmet wood-fired pizza and a bottle of [the beer] Stella Artois? And what if the overweight person was a well-known playwright and bon vivant who just happened to be watching a 24-hour Shakespeare festival?

Television Is Neutral

It's very difficult to have rational discussions about television because an emotive script condemning it has been so thoroughly written. TV has become a symbol of all that's allegedly wrong with the modern world. It has come to embody our fears that families no longer communicate properly, that we only work to fill up our lives with meaningless consumer goods and that we're hooked on instant gratification. These are all claims that deserve thoughtful discussions. But putting television on trial won't get us very far.

Television is something a lot of people use in very benign ways. They use it to relax in the evening after a hard day's work. And the majority of us are working harder and harder and doing it in a world that is increasingly complex and demanding. Even so, relaxing and tuning out is not something we're told we should do. On the contrary, we're exhorted by the life coaches, psychologists and motivational speakers who populate the media to be endlessly productive and in constant meaningful communication with work colleagues, clients and loved ones. If you're going to relax, then the productive way to do it is to haul yourself off to an advanced yoga class or go and pound the pavement at the local park. Watching television is just too much of a simple pleasure. It's not demanding anything of us. We're not producing anything by doing it. We're not improving ourselves. Anyone spot the ghost of the Protestant work ethic lurking behind the screen?

Television, in other words, is carrying the can for a lot of anxieties it has little to do with. The reality is that television is in itself a relatively neutral medium. You can watch highbrow documentaries on it, you can wallow in a weekend festival of Elvis [Presley] movies, beer and pizza, you can fall in love with Grace Kelly in *Rear Window* [a highly acclaimed movie by Alfred Hitchcock] all over again or you can check the weather before you take the kids to the park. In real life, television is part of the furniture. It's useful. It's entertaining. It helps us unwind. Children's television is frequently highly educational as well as relaxing and entertaining for them. How many people do you know, when you really think about it, who resemble the stereotypical television viewer—slack-jawed, empty-brained, obese, staring blankly at the box in the corner? Most of us are far too busy for that. In fact, the heaviest viewers of television are not kids or young people or even families. It's older people, people who've retired; people who have time and probably have very strong opinions about what they see on TV.

The reality is that television in itself is a relatively neutral medium.

Moral Panics

But reality is besides the point when a moral panic is under way. And the moral panic over television has been under way periodically for some fifty years now. When you throw children and obesity into that mix you have the recipe for one of the biggest moral panics of all time.

The ABC (America) News Web site reported recently on two conflicting studies that were both published in the *Journal of the American Medical Association.* One had found some evidence of a simple cause-and-effect relationship between TV viewing and teenagers' body-fat levels and another did not, preferring to look at broader issues like class, gender, race, education level and fears about neighbourhood safety. But this didn't stop the report being filed under the panic headline 'Girls and Minority Kids on the TV Fat Track.'

In May 2005, the *Australian* ran a story by its medical reporter under the headline 'Children Grow Fat on TV Diet.' Or do they? The article actually concerned an Australian Institute of Family Studies report warning that kids who spent more time watching television than exercising were more likely to eat high-fat food than fruit and vegetables. That's all. The problem was the food their parents provided for them—not the television they were watching. The report also found that kids aged four and five spent just over two hours each day watching TV, videos or DVDs. Again the silence on the broader issues of parental diets, class, gender, education level and fears about neighbourhood safety was deafening.

The problem was the food their parents provided for them—not the television they were watching.

A Web site for Australia's general practitioners, myDr.com .au, made the TV-obesity link in 2003: 'Australia has an obesity epidemic and it has been strongly linked to how much time people spend watching television.' The article looked at the results of an Australian diabetes, obesity and lifestyle study, published in the *Medical Journal of Australia.* However, what the study really found was that it was a combination of eating high-energy foods, lack of exercise and too much sedentary activity that led to weight problems. And think about it: Wouldn't sedentary activities include not just watching TV, but also working at a computer, reading a book, playing the piano, going to the opera or lying on the grass watching the clouds float by? And what about other factors—the diets of parents, for instance? Wouldn't that impact on child obesity? And aren't there socioeconomic factors at play as well? So the facts show that TV is not the culprit at all.

If there's a panic about childhood going around, you can bet Young Media Australia [YMA] won't miss that bus. [Its] Web site has a downloadable brochure on TV and obesity which deemed the situation urgent enough to demand the language of warfare. 'More than one in four Australian children are overweight!' the brochure warned. 'Keep your children out of the firing line!' YMA also urged parents: 'Don't let preschoolers watch any commercial TV at all. If your children are older, wean them away from commercial TV. Watch the ABC. Teach your children to hit the "mute" button whenever an ad appears!'

The YMA approach is to treat the TV like it's some kind of thermonuclear device that has to be disarmed, sort of like Sean Connery foiling Goldfinger's plan to detonate a bomb inside Fort Knox. Of course, YMA wouldn't let you or your kids see *Goldfinger* [a famous spy movie starring Sean Connery as James Bond], or any other James Bond movie for that matter, but you get the point.

TV Is Not Linked to Inactivity

We've seen a parade of people and organisations who have desperately searched for a simple direct link between the amount of TV you and your children watch and how fat you all are. And we've seen that even if they can't find a direct link—and they can't—they want to act as if there is one. But has anyone ever shown there is no link, or moved beyond the cathode-ray tube in the corner and looked at broader issues? As a matter of fact, yes.

In 2005, Sydney's *Sun-Herald* reported that research by the Australian Bureau of Statistics, 'showed that children who played sports or danced also watched between 10 and 20 hours a week of television and played an average of seven hours a week of computer games. The Internet was not a problem either as children were even more likely to be active if they had access to a computer at home.'

The study's author, Mike Stratton, noted, 'There's no doubt that screen-based activities do compete for a child's time. But if you want to look at the reasons why they are really not participating [in sports], it's more to do with socioeconomics.' The report found that the most reliable indicator for whether a child did not play sports was that the parents were unemployed. The next most reliable factors? Parents born in a non-English-speaking country, and having low socioeconomic status.

The amount of time spent watching television or computer games was either not significant to or only slightly influenced rates of sporting activity.

The amount of time spent watching television ... was either not significant to or only slightly influenced rates of sporting activity.

But perhaps the study with the greatest impact on the debate has come from America's Kaiser Family Foundation, a nonprofit, private operating foundation dedicated to providing information and analysis on health care issues. Their 2004 report, *The Role of Media in Childhood Obesity*, was a review of more than 40 studies on the role of media in America's child weight problem. It showed that there was only weak evidence at best to link sedentary TV watching with being overweight or obese. In fact, kids who watch less TV might just be replacing TV time with other sedentary activities like reading books and playing board games.

It also showed that just because your kids might watch TV, that didn't mean they'd also be less likely to race down to the park after the show to ride their bikes.

The report, then, was all for sedentary activity. And we say, what's so wrong about lying around doing nothing occasionally? Equally, the Kaiser study found that the media was able to play a positive role in helping to reduce childhood weight issues, through programs that encourage children to be active and help teach good nutrition, and through public education campaigns.

The report also emphasised the fact that media (whether it be the mere fact of watching TV or exposure to advertising) was just one part of a very complex jigsaw puzzle. For example, the report notes that the U.S. Centers for Disease Control and Prevention found that while 10 per cent of 2–5-year-olds and 15 per cent of 6–19-year-olds are overweight, the numbers skyrocket among Mexican American and African American children. In other words, once again, childhood obesity, can be said to be a political, economic or social problem as much as a medical one.

Similar findings were made by Dr Michael Gard of Charles Sturt University and Professor Jan Wright of the University of Wollongong in their book *The Obesity Epidemic*, published in 2005. This was another review of all the scientific literature on obesity. They report that kids who use technology like TV and computers the most are 'actually more likely, not less likely, to be physically active, and that claims about TV causing obesity are simply not based on fact. They come from age-old anxieties over technology.' For Gard and Wright, the whole debate over TV and obesity is driven by an unspoken cultural prejudice that regards overweight people as lazy and stupid.

According to Dr Gard, speaking in the London *Daily Telegraph*: 'Science has got to stop looking for simple answers, because obesity is not a simple problem.'

A Convenient Villain

TV is the easy villain in the piece, the man in the black hat who we can all jeer, the social ill that everyone can smugly de-

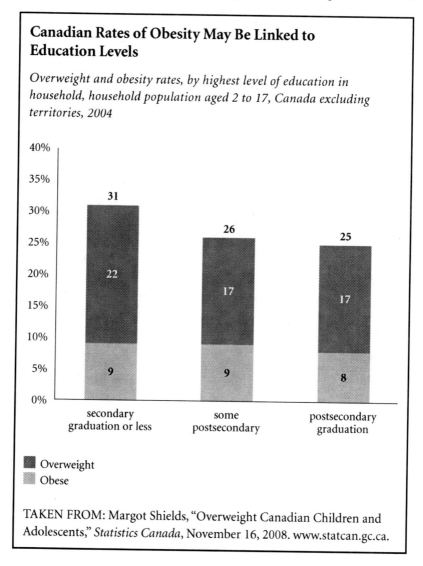

Canadian Rates of Obesity May Be Linked to Education Levels

Overweight and obesity rates, by highest level of education in household, household population aged 2 to 17, Canada excluding territories, 2004

■ Overweight
▨ Obese

TAKEN FROM: Margot Shields, "Overweight Canadian Children and Adolescents," *Statistics Canada*, November 16, 2008. www.statcan.gc.ca.

nounce. After all, TV is the great invention of modern life, and modern life (we just assume, without knowing why) must be easier or softer than life in the world of our grandfathers. In fact, TV and the obesity crisis are the hand and glove of moral panics in the modern world.

There can be no greater example of sanctimonious moralising than in the case of Greg Critser, a left-wing American journalist, and his 2003 book, with the take-no-prisoners title of *Fat Land: How Americans Became the Fattest People in the World*. Critser, who was diagnosed as obese in 1998 and lost weight with the help of prescription drugs, told London's *Observer* newspaper in 2003:

> Most of us are fat because we are slothful and gluttonous. People don't want to hear that. In the course of researching my book, I came to believe that, morally, overeating is wrong. Look at [Hieronymus] Bosch's depiction of gluttony: a man is eating; his child is tugging at his shirt; another man sits at the end of the table with nothing on his plate; his wife is waiting at the door for his next demand. Act the glutton, and you're not only worshipping your belly as a false god; you're involved in the dereliction of your secular duties as well. You're not taking care of your child; you're taking the food off somebody else's plate; you're neglecting your duties at work; you're not taking care of your body.

Morally, overeating is wrong. Doesn't that take us all the way back to the death of that three-year-old in London with the eating problem caused by a genetic disorder? [In 2004, a child with a genetic disorder that caused her to overeat died; the media reported her death as the result of poor parenting and sloth.] Was she to blame, morally? Did she deserve it?

TV is the easy villain in the piece, the man in the black hat who we can all jeer, the social ill that everyone can smugly denounce.

Julia Baird, writing in the *Sydney Morning Herald* in 2004, quoted Paul Campos in his book *The Obesity Myth*: 'If one were forced to come up with a six-word explanation for the otherwise inexplicable ferocity of America's war on fat, it would be this: Americans think being fat is disgusting.'

Fifty years ago, he argues,

America was full of people that the social elites could look upon with something approaching open disgust: blacks in particular, of course, but also other ethnic minorities, the poor, women, Jews, homosexuals, and so on. Nowadays, a new target is required ... on average, poor people in America are fat and rich people are thin. The disgust the thin upper classes feel for the fat lower classes has nothing to do with mortality statistics and everything to do with feelings of moral superiority.

And as Polly Toynbee wrote in the *Guardian* in 2004: 'It is inequality and disrespect that make people fat.... People will only get thinner when they are included in things that are worth staying thin for. Offer self-esteem, respect, jobs or some social status and the pounds would start to fall away.' This exactly echoes what Dr [Jenny] O'Dea found in her research at Sydney University.

So forget about TV for a moment. Could it be, do you think—perverse as it might sound—that the moral panic about child obesity might be one of the causes of child obesity? If you'll pardon the expression, it's certainly food for thought.

Western Pornography and Culture Encourage Genital Plastic Surgery Among Women

Suzy Freeman-Greene

Suzy Freeman-Greene is a senior writer at the Australian news-paper the Age. In the following viewpoint, she argues that the mainstreaming of pornography and "raunch" culture in the United States, Australia, and Britain have made many women anxious about the shapes of their vaginas. This has resulted in an increase in genital plastic surgery, which Freeman-Greene argues is expensive, unnecessary, and potentially dangerous.

As you read, consider the following questions:

1. What are some of the potential damaging effects of la-bioplasty according to Freeman-Greene?
2. Kourosh Tavakoli says that his patients request labio-plasty for what reasons?
3. According to Ted Weaver, what should people be taught in sex education classes in high school?

[U].S. pop singer] Britney Spears' singing prowess may be deeply suspect but she can thrust her genitals at a camera with aplomb. The video for her new song "3" is full of pelvic-led career moves, variously delivered in a tight, white bathing suit and a black, G-stringed affair.

Pressure to Conform

An ability to dance like a stripper seems depressingly necessary for many of today's female pop stars, with videos virtually shot from the floor up. This new focus on women's genitalia is mirrored elsewhere in pop culture, with suburban pole dancing classes and Brazilian waxes [the removal of pubic hair with the use of wax] that impose a prepubescent beauty ideal on adult parts.

With female genitals on display like never before, there's bizarre new pressure on them to conform to a uniform look. Recently, ABC News reported on concerns about the popularity of vaginal plastic surgery. More than 1200 Australian women a year are said to undergo a procedure known as labioplasty, which trims and reshapes the labia minora [two folds on women's external genitals].

Dr Ted Weaver, president of the Royal Australian and NZ [New Zealand] College of Obstetricians and Gynaecologists, told me he believes this figure grossly underestimates the number of women getting "designer vaginas". Such surgery, he says, is dangerous, costly and largely unnecessary. (In rare cases, it may be medically required). Labioplasty can have damaging after effects including scarring, infection and painful sex. And despite the claims on some cosmetic surgery Web sites, he says there's no evidence it will improve your sex life.

Such surgery is dangerous, costly and largely unnecessary.

Weaver believes labioplasty often preys on women's feelings of insecurity. Doctors should instead be trained to explain to them that genital appearance can vary greatly and surgery is not the answer. "She doesn't have to conform to a picture that she might have noticed in a girlie magazine."

Labioplasty can cost anything from $4000 to $10,000. Plastic surgeon Dr Kourosh Tavakoli told ABC he had been performing it for seven years, with the number of patients doubling annually. He blames less qualified practitioners, such as "GP surgeons" working in their poorly lit offices, for most health problems linked to the procedure. Eighty per cent of his clients have had a labioplasty for "cosmetic and psychological reasons"—chiefly discomfort during sex or being unable "to wear a leotard or (swimming) cossie". The procedure, he claims, can bring about "a mental transformation".

Anxiety and Confusion

It seems astounding that women would endure such pain and cost merely to look subtly different in a leotard. Far more plausible is a link between the widespread availability of porn [pornography], the popularity of Brazilians [genitalia waxes] and the growth of labioplasty. Left to their natural hirsute state, how many people would even notice the shape of their genitals?

A recent article in the *British Journal of Obstetrics and Gynaecology* reported on a qualitative study of six women who'd had labioplasty. (In Britain, the incidence of this surgery has doubled in the past five years.) All felt as if their original genital appearance was odd. Yet most revealed uncertainty about what "normal" women's genitalia should look like.

All felt as if their original genital appearance was odd. Yet most revealed uncertainty about what "normal" women's genitalia should look like.

The women reported anxiety about their sexual partners seeing or touching their genitals. While some spoke of discomfort, the authors noted that this, rather than appearance, might be emphasised as a way of legitimising their request for surgery. After the procedure, the women were less self-conscious, but their expectations of better sex were not necessarily met.

Importantly, the authors noted that the vagina is often negatively represented in wider culture and depicted as "a viable site for beautification and normalisation". Women's magazines "present a social norm that women's genitalia should be invisible and that there should be a smooth curve between the thighs with no protruding labia".

Raunch culture has a lot to answer for here. And as the shape of the vagina becomes a crazy new source of angst, we still don't even have an affectionate word to describe it. Where is the cosy, non-threatening equivalent to "willy" [a slang term for penis]? This linguistic absence speaks volumes about social attitudes towards female genitalia. Meanwhile, the c-word endures as a form of abuse.

Weaver thinks genital appearance should be taught in high school sex education classes. People need to know, he says, that there are as many different labial shapes as there are nose sizes.

It's hard not to see a further irony in this disturbing trend. While women overseas are often powerless to resist genital mutilation [in some nations in Asia and Africa, young girls may have their external genital organs removed as part of coming-of-age rituals], women here [in the West] are paying for surgery that may be harmful or utterly superfluous.

In Russia, Television Has Increased the Popularity of Police

Elena Baraban

Elena Baraban is a professor at the University of Manitoba. In the following viewpoint, she argues that after the Soviet era, police were generally held in low esteem in Russia. They were seen as corrupt, violent, and untrustworthy. The television show Streets of Broken Lights *managed to raise respect for the police by showing them in a humorous but sympathetic way.*

As you read, consider the following questions:

1. According to Baraban, why was *Streets of Broken Lights* not originally called *The Cops*?

2. In the popular imagination of post-Soviet popular culture, what did policemen become associated with, according to Baraban?

3. Baraban says that the protagonists of Soviet detective fiction sincerely believed in what?

On January 1, 1998, the TNT channel [a Russian network] began broadcasting a new detective series *Streets of Broken Lights (Ulitsy razbitykh fonarei)*. The show became an in-

Elena Baraban, "A Reconciling Smile: Humor in the Detective Series *Streets of Broken Lights*," in *Uncensored? Reinventing Humor and Satire in Post-Soviet Russia*, edited by Olga Mesropova and Seth Graham, Winnipeg, MB: Slavica Publishers, 2008, pp. 145–159. Copyright © 2008 by Elena Baraban. Reproduced by permission of the author.

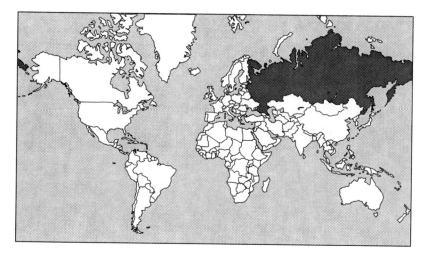

stant success and was subsequently run on ORT and later on NTV, Russia's two main television channels. The program earned the reputation of *narodnyi serial* (people's show) and received prestigious awards including two TEFI [an annual award given by the Russian television industry] awards in 1999 for best television project of the year and for best series. Confirming the view of popular culture as an active historical force, *Streets* had an outstanding social impact: its cast members received a prize "For resurrecting people's love for the police," high school graduates began to enroll en masse in *militsiia* [police] colleges, and children played *menty* [cop] games. In 1997, when Alexander Rogozhkin, the director of the series' first episode, suggested the whole series be called *The Cops* (*Menty*), producer Alexander Kapitsa considered the title inappropriate, for at that time the word had a distinctly negative connotation. However, in its second season, the series acquired the subtitle *The Cops' New Adventures (Novye prikliucheniia mentov)* and its sequels have become better known by the subtitles *The Cops-3, The Cops-4*, etc., than by the original title *Streets of Broken Lights*. As the actor Sergei Selin suggests, thanks to *Streets*, the word *ment* (cop) is no longer an insult in Russia. . . .

Humor Made the Police Popular

If one is to consider the secret of *Streets'* success in the end of the 1990s, a decade that witnessed a veritable detective boom in Russian culture, a reference to successful story lines and characters would not be enough to explain the popularity of this particular series. It was the heroes' humorous outlook on life in Russia that set *Streets* apart from many Soviet and post-Soviet *detektivy* [detective stories] and ensured the reputation of the series. Humor was essential for making each episode of *Streets* not only an engaging narrative about a particular criminal investigation but also a commentary on post-Soviet Russia [that is, Russia since 1991, when the Communist regime fell], a commentary that appealed to various audiences, reconciled different ideological positions and thus helped renegotiate the public's attitude towards the police. In this regard it is not accidental that reviews of the show, interviews with its original producer and actors as well as scholarly articles invariably mention the use of humor in *Streets*. In a 2001 interview producer Alexander Kapitsa said that the show's plots would always include gags and jokes that *chernukha* (relentlessly negative depictions of life in Russia during the *glasnost* period [the second half of the 1980s, just before the fall of communism]) would be transformed into black humor. In fact, beginning with *Streets* (1998–2004), humor, which had been used rather sparingly in the Russian *detektiv*, became a prominent narrative strategy not only in the police procedural but also in tales of private investigations that formed the subgenre *ironicheskii detektiv* (ironic detective novel). . . .

Not Soviet Villains

Much of the humor in *Streets* is inter-textual, contrasting the protagonists of the series with negative images of the police in post-Soviet popular culture while ultimately subverting these images. Indeed, when transgressions of legality among the police came to light in the *glasnost* period and official law enforcement was implicated in numerous publications exposing Stalinism,[1] the police lost public respect. The generally negative image of the police in post-Soviet popular culture is exemplified by jokes about the police (*anekdoty pro mentov*). In the popular imagination a policeman became associated with a *ment* or *musor* (lit. "garbage") who is rude with witnesses, takes bribes, collaborates with criminals, and beats suspects. Instead of suppressing infractions of legality by the police and thus compromising the authenticity of the show, the producers of *Streets* make sure that the protagonists both address and subvert negative stereotypes of the police. It is clear that the heroes of *Streets* know about the accusations, which are leveled against the police, particularly accusations of corruption and abuse of power. A jar on the cops' desk reads "For bribes," and torture equipment is prominently displayed in the office whenever the cops deal with a stubborn suspect or uncooperative witnesses. However, these props are never used by the heroes of *Streets* in the way one would expect them to be used by cops depicted in *anekdoty*. In the series these props serve a dual function: They alert the audience's memory to negative stereotypes of the police and, at the same time, expose these stereotypes as false. According to psychologist Jacob Levine, humor may serve as protection from "the destructive aggression" of others: "Individuals often suffer extreme reactions of shame when they are publicly laughed at, but not when they are under the protective cloak of the humor illusion." It is only logical then that the creators of *Streets* make their protagonists adopt a humorous attitude to public criticism of the police. For example, when Captain Vladimir Kazantsev, one of the show's protagonists, sees that a witness is afraid to testify on the grounds that the police would do nothing to protect her, he exclaims theatrically: "Ah! I am going to be late for an appointment at the Godfather's. . . . Today's payday!" Then he

---

1. Joseph Stalin ruled Russia from 1922–1953 and was responsible for massive state-sponsored violence and repression.

humorously explains how he and his comrades do a lot of things "for free": For example, they get wounded or killed while trying to protect the innocent. Here the detective's self-reflexive and somewhat bitter humor works as a defamiliarization tool, through undermining the expectations of the audience and making the audience conscious of its unfair assumptions. As philosopher Simon Critchley reminds us, "Jokes tear holes in our usual perception about the empirical world. We might say that humor is produced by a disjunction between the way things are and the way they are represented in the joke, between expectation and actuality. Humor defeats our expectations by producing a novel actuality, by changing the situation in which we find ourselves."

It was the heroes' humorous outlook on life in Russia that set Streets *apart.*

Perfect Heroes

Humor is also used inter-textually when the heroes of *Streets* are implicitly contrasted with the heroes of Soviet *detektivy*. The basis for this contrast is the detectives' attitude towards their work and their understanding of their role in society. The fundamentally serious detective of Soviet *detektivy* believed that this work made important demands on him. He was actively engaged in eliminating disturbances of the familiar order of things. In addition to incorporating such universal qualities of the detective as honesty, valor, and devotion to maintaining order in society, the image of a Soviet police detective also conformed to socialist ideology. In Soviet popular culture detectives defined themselves as citizens who took an active part in building socialism. In Grigori Kokhan's *Born by the Revolution (Rozhdennaia revoliutsiei*, 1974–77), Alexander Faintsimmer's *Tavern in Piatnitsky Street (Traktir na Piatnitskoi*, 1977), and Stanislav Govorukhin's *The Meeting Place Cannot Be Changed (Mesto vstrechi izmenit nelzia* 1979), the protagonists sincerely believed in the ultimate victory of Communist ideals and dreamed of a future in which their profession would be unnecessary because there would be no crime. They enthusiastically worked towards eliminating criminal activity in Russia and, despite serious obstacles in their path such as economic stagnation, "counterrevolution," wars, or poor materiel [equipment], they had no doubt they would be able to ensure the triumph of good. Given the pathos of the Soviet *detektiv*, there was little room for humor in its depictions of the police. . . .

The ironic, slightly cynical detectives of Streets *are not perfect. Nor do they aspire to be.*

Unlike their Soviet predecessors, who were shown as men of achievement, as individuals who embraced the idea of progress both at work and in their private lives, the ironic, slightly cynical detectives of *Streets* are not perfect. Nor do they aspire to be. Because their weaknesses are acknowledged, they appear to be more authentic heroes than their Soviet predecessors. By showing the detectives as "smaller" heroes and by exposing their imperfections, *Streets* highlights problems typical of post-Soviet society: the necessity of coming to terms with Russia's controversial past and its uncertain present. Humor helps the heroes to develop a new perspective on their society's problems. At the end of the 1990s, it seems, the fantasy detectives stopped perceiving society as merely distressing and began to view the incongruities of life in Russia as amusing, as a playful reorganization of life. Such a change to perspective indicates a certain level of comfort on the part of these characters with the new Russia. In turn, this new level of comfort that the heroes feel with regard to society (and with regard to their limited capabilities to deal with all their challenges) explains why the show has become so popular. To a certain extent the detectives' humorous stance vis-à-vis Russia and their own role in post-Soviet Russia makes these characters believable and likeable, and thereby rehabilitates the police for the Russian viewer.

Northeastern Thailand Has Gained a More Positive Image Because of Its Music

Terry Miller

Terry Miller is an ethnomusicologist and a retired professor of Kent State University. In the following viewpoint, he argues that the northeastern Isan region of Thailand has long been stereo- typed as an undesirable rural backwater. However, in recent years, Isan music has been updated and has become very suc- cessful with people from all over Thailand and beyond. Large- scale concerts by Isan performers focusing on Isan themes are a major attraction, even in sophisticated urban areas like Bangkok. As a result of these changes, images of the Isan region have be- come much more positive.

As you read, consider the following questions:

1. What is *lam klawn?*

2. According to Miller, what professions in Bangkok have Isan natives traditionally dominated?

Terry Miller, "From Country Hick to Rural Hip: A New Identity Through Music for Northeast Thailand," *Asian Music*, vol. 36, no. 2, Summer 2005, pp. 96–103, 105–106. Copyright © 2005 by the University of Texas Press. Reproduced by permission of the publisher and the author.

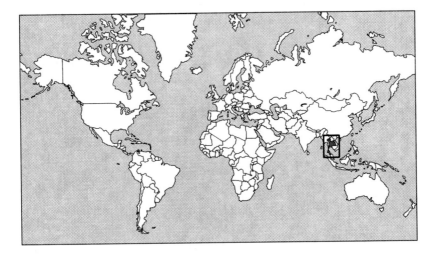

3. What does Miller say is the main difference between a *luk thung* show and a *lam sing*?

Thailand's northeast region, known in Thai as Isan, consists of nineteen provinces out of the country's total of seventy-six and approximately one-third of its total population of 62 million. Of the country's four regions—the others being the central plain, the north, and the south—Isan has long had the most problematic image. When I arrived in Thailand in 1972 to begin my doctoral dissertation study of Isan music, at a point when development of the region was only beginning, Isan's reputation was decidedly negative. Upon telling Thai friends that we were going to live in the northeast, we were strongly encouraged to reconsider. They told me the region was extremely hot, poor, and undeveloped, the people were lazy, stupid, and dirty, and the food smelled bad. Bangkok [the capital of Thailand] flourished then, as it does now, on the cheap labor of Isan migrants, especially as maids, taxi drivers, and laborers. Better to keep the family in (civilized) Bangkok and make short visits to Isan for research material. Roger Crutchley, whose columns in the *Bangkok Post* reflected a colonial-style "expat" sensibility, wrote the following about his time in Yasothon province visiting the home of his maid:

"All in all, we had a typically hectic Isan schedule—sleep, get up, eat chicken, doze, eat more chicken, drink, doze, try a bit of chicken. These people in Isan aren't stupid."

They told me the region was extremely hot, poor, and undeveloped, the people were lazy, stupid, and dirty, and the food smelled bad.

Isan Transformed

Elsewhere in Thailand, Isan music was little-known and poorly understood. While the free-reed mouth organ called *khaen* was pleasant enough to listen to, no one outside Isan could make much sense of the seemingly interminable texts sung in Isan dialect, a regional form of Lao, by the *maw lam* singers who performed from dusk to dawn for villagers seated on the cold, hard ground. While the Isan language is part of the Thai language family, the texts are replete with local cultural allusions and double entendres opaque to non-native speakers. And Isan culture was considered to be as lowbrow as you could get in Thailand.

It is my contention that the profound changes that have come to Isan over the past thirty years, including to its music and theater, not only obliterated much of what was considered "traditional" in earlier times but changed the way the rest of Thailand viewed Isan. As its entertainments modernized and expanded, they took the country by storm and have come to dominate the popular music scene. With the exception of Bangkok, where most modern entertainments naturally begin, the rest of Thailand could mount no response as effective as that of Isan, resulting in the latter's music and theater coming to be seen as the "coolest in the kingdom." As a result, the public perception of Isan and its people has been transformed from "country hick" to "rural hip." Since Isan music has attained a higher cultural profile than anything else from the region, it has been the primary engine for changing negative perceptions to positive ones. . . .

The public perception of Isan has been transformed from "country hick" to "rural hip."

Musical Changes

The old Isan musical culture that baffled people from outside the region was dominated by repartee vocal genres generally known as *lam*. By the early 1970s several archaic *lam* genres had already become scarce, leaving the repartee form called *lam klawn* ("poetry singing") dominant. Originally performed outdoors on the ground by alternating male and female singers accompanied by the region's chief instrument, the *khaen* (a raft-form free-reed mouth organ with sixteen pipes), *lam klawn* began about 9 P.M. and lasted until dawn. Performed in conjunction with both calendrical and Buddhist festivals, *lam* was locally sponsored, simply staged, and free to the community. Its texts, sophisticated poetry replete with double entendres and cultural allusions, ranged from a feigned love affair between the singers to didactic texts on Buddhism, history, geography, and literature. These were presented in three clearly demarcated segments: *lam thang san*, which was metrical, used a "major"-sounding pentatonic scale [a scale common to much folk music], and lasted through most of the night; *lam thang nyao*, which was non-metrical, used a "minor"-sounding pentatonic scale, and was sad in emotion; and *lam toei*, which was metrical (often described as danceable), "minor"-sounding, and upbeat. The last two sections might comprise only an hour or less in total. . . .

Lam klawn was sometimes heard outside Isan, primarily in Bangkok, because a significant percentage of that city's population has long consisted of both permanent and temporary laborers who have migrated from overpopulated and chronically impoverished Isan. Although laborers from the north and south also migrate to Bangkok, the Isan people dominate several professions, especially as maids, gardeners, and taxi drivers. To a lesser extent they also work in factories and sometimes in Thailand's notorious flesh trade. Most came to Bangkok knowing they would have to live in modest surroundings, even slums, but their access to income would far exceed that available in the Isan rice, jute, tapioca, and tobacco fields. Since the northeast is more likely to suffer droughts and floods than is the rest of Thailand, and its rice crop is glutinous rice (eaten by both Lao and Isan people but also the raw material for Thai whiskey), the only thing guaranteed in Isan was its endemic poverty.

Thailand's economy was in a state of rapid growth during the last thirty years of the twentieth century, and workers in Bangkok flourished, increasingly able to purchase and enjoy the fruits of modernization. Great numbers of Isan people living in modernizing Bangkok and experiencing its entertainments and media thus came to have more "sophisticated" tastes than did their relatives who stayed behind in the villages. When they returned home for the holidays, these primarily young workers who now lived under the bright lights of the city wanted updated entertainments as well, no longer being attracted to the small-scale, low-key, and old-fashioned performances preferred by their aging parents and grandparents. As *lam* became more and more market-driven, the performers had to respond. The scale to which this is happening is easily seen during long holiday weekends, when the traffic from Bangkok to the northeast is bumper-to-bumper and several Isan provinces attain the highest rates of auto accidents in the country.

A Challenge to Traditional Isan Performers

Old-fashioned Isan performers also faced another challenge, the rise of the *luk thung* popular song. Thai popular song developed primarily in Bangkok in the 1940s, much of it based on the Anglo-American ballroom dance music then popular among the upper (and Westernized) class. These slow, often sentimental, songs were called *phleng luk krung* (literally, "child of the city" songs). It is difficult to date the origin of the *phleng luk thung* (literally, "child of the field"), but its roots go back at least into the 1950s. By the time I arrived in 1972, *luk thung* songs were beginning to take off but were hardly dominant. Based to some extent on the regional musics of the northeast, north, and south, and sometimes sung by singers who came from traditional performance, these "country songs" expressed the experiences of rural peoples, both farmers laboring in virtually premodern villages and the migrant Isan workers living in Bangkok's slums and working for pittances to keep the city running smoothly. Over time, northeastern-derived *luk thung* songs came to dominate and, because the Isan population was so large, came to have commercial potential. First marketed on five-inch vinyl recordings and later on audio cassette, *phleng luk thung* also came to dominate the airwaves, and certain singers, such as Pompuang Duangjan and Suraphon Sombatjalern, attained star status. Later, Thai MTV featured *luk thung* videos, and a radio station devoted to this genre began broadcasting around the clock in 1997.

When they returned home for the holidays, these primarily young workers who now lived under the bright lights of the city wanted updated entertainments as well.

Luk thung songs are most often performed live in large-scale open-air concerts featuring powerful sound systems, bright lights, troupes of dancing young women who change their Las Vegas-style floor-show costumes for each song, several fashionably attired star singers, and a live rock/jazz combo that may include a traditional instrument or two, although more for looks than for sound. Whether or not Western or upper-class Thai observers find these events to be sophisticated, *luk thung* shows are among the most energetic and colorful going in Thailand today. Because virtually all *luk thung* are Isan-derived and focus on the lives of rice farmers and their descendents, they have raised Isan's profile to a prominent level and, since the songs are extremely popular, they give the region's image a lively, up-to-date makeover.

Because virtually all luk thung *are Isan-derived and focus on the lives of rice farmers and their descendents, they have raised Isan's profile to a prominent level.*

The significance of the genre of *luk thung* songs is suggested by the amount of space it receives in John Clewley's article on Thailand in the two-volume edition of *World Music: The Rough Guide*. Of the six photos in the article, four feature Isan music making, three of them in modernized forms. Material on Isan genres, both traditional and modern, comprises around two-thirds of the text. Evidently "ex-pat" Clewley, who lives in Bangkok, sees Isan music, especially the *luk thung*, as virtually dominating the music scene. His enthusiastic comments suggest that Isan music is the best show in town....

New Musical Genres in Isan

Other factors were helping to facilitate these changes. Not only had the highway and media systems penetrated Isan totally, bringing Bangkok's popular culture with them, but the education system was also expanding. Although regional universities now included research institutes devoted to the study of local culture, they otherwise reflected modern pan-Thai culture in their use of central Thai language, the dominance of "national" concepts over regional ones (such as in history, geography, literature, and the arts), and the fact that the students were also tuned into this modern Thai world....

By the end of the 1980s, with *lam klawn* repartee singing wheezing for its last breath of air, something had to be done

Singer Christy Gibson Discusses Technique

One thing about lukthoong [luk thung] is that the singing style is extremely expressive. My first lukthoong teacher said ... frequently in the beginning that "... *you must capture the feeling of the lyrics of the song*". Of course that's true of all singing in pretty much any language, but as a foreigner [Gibson is Dutch-British.] I found this much more difficult to do when singing in Thai, as it's not my first language.

The lyrics of lukthoong songs, particularly the older and more classic ones, are very beautiful and poetic and are often not in what you would call "spoken Thai". Thus it was a challenge for me to be able to really capture the essence and feeling of what was being said. . . .

The tones of the words in the songs also direct the melody to a very large degree. . . . Naturally, that is the case as Thai is a tonal language, but it is, obviously, very different from singing in English where you can improvise quite a bit so long as you are singing on key and within the chords, etc. That only works in Thai so long as you are improvising within the tones of a given word.

Christy Gibson, as told to Catherine Wentworth,
"Expat Interview: Jonas Anderson and Christy Gibson,"
Women Learning Thai ... And Some Men Too Blog,
December 9, 2009. http://womenlearnthai.com.

or old-fashioned Isan singing would be engulfed by the *luk thung* phenomenon. Whether or not Ms Ratri Sriwilai of Khon Kaen actually created the genre, which she claims to have done with her brother around 1989, she has been a leading force in making *lam sing* Thailand's rage of the 1990s and beyond. *Sing* means "racing," or anything fast. Ratri and others, deciding to fight fire with fire, created a hot new genre that brings together traditional repartee and *khaen* accompaniment with energetic dancing, *luk thung* songs, "hip" costumes, and the accompaniment of electric *phin* lute and drum kit. The *lam sing* firestorm engulfed all Thailand. Not only were non-Isan audiences listening to *lam sing*, some of whose texts were actually in the central Thai language, but the performers of many other genres around the country felt compelled to go "*sing*" as well. A wildly enthusiastic Thai youth culture embraced this up-to-date form of country music, virtually eliminating the old *lam klawn* and even threatening the *luk thung* troupes. Ratri's *maw lam sing* school at her home in Khon Kaen continues to attract dozens of Isan youth looking for glamour and excitement. *Lam sing* had what Thailand's youth were seeking: high decibel output, colorful costumes, frenetic activity, and pop music—along with a good portion of "tradition."

Lam sing blended segments of traditional *lam* with *luk thung* songs and created its own order of events. Whereas the dance that went with the old *lam* was slow and graceful, *lam sing* dance is energetic, jerky, and sometimes suggestive. Even the *khaen* player is expected to dance while playing. Some *luk thung* songs are sung in central Thai, and indeed, there has been a steady decline in the use of the Isan dialect by the younger generation. A number of *lam sing* performers besides Ratri have become stars and appear in videos, on VCDs [a cheap video format common in Asia], and on television. Many were originally her students. Since only males normally play *khaen*, it is odd to see Ratri's otherwise very quiet and modest daughter play *khaen* with the troupe, dancing as energetically as any male player.

To the uninitiated, a *lam sing* performance may be difficult to differentiate from a *luk thung* show, or from the first few hours of a *lam mu* or *lam ploen* performance. The stages are equally large, the accompanying musicians include both Western and Isan instruments, some electrified, the costumes are the same and, in some cases, the songs are the same. But *lam sing* omits the troupes of dancing women. Clearly, then, such spectacles offer the musical formula that appeals to today's audiences. At any festival, whether it celebrates something of Isan or all of Thailand, one can be sure that the groups on the Isan stages will be the biggest, brightest, loudest, and most energetic. Not surprisingly, the Isan stages are also the hardest to get close to, because they attract the largest audiences. . . .

Lam sing *had what Thailand's youth were seeking: high decibel output, colorful costumes, frenetic activity, and pop music—along with a good portion of "tradition."*

A Positive Image

Just how far Isan culture has come in making the transition from "hick" to "hip" was noted during a recent visit. Isan food is now typical "mall food" and we saw one sit-down restaurant featuring Italian and Isan food. McDonald's was not just offering an Isan green papaya salad (called *somtam*) in the "salad shaker" style but had created a pork sandwich using Isan sticky rice pressed into buns. Perhaps the most remarkable change that is now progressing is a revivalism of old-style Isan music led by a completely traditional, blind *khaen* player named Sombat Simla. Sombat has become a minor cult figure, performing for young central Thai audiences in a somewhat American-style folk festival format, sometimes including an old-fashioned *lam klawn* singer. This is a new trend that bears careful watching.

The image of Isan has clearly undergone massive changes since the early 1970s. This is most obvious in the dramatic rise and success of several modernized genres, whose "in your face" aggressiveness celebrates Thailand's growing and affluent youth culture. Unfortunately for traditionalists, these entertainments project an urbanized, raucous, escapist vision of

Isan, rather than the more introspective side formerly heard in *lam klawn* singing, reflecting on Buddhism, literature, history, proper behavior, courtship, and the life of farmers toiling in the rice fields. . . . The projected image of Isan has become a positive one that connects with people outside Isan. True, Isan is still not the destination of choice for Thai seeking greener pastures, nor has migration to Bangkok slowed, but at least the Isan people living there and elsewhere no longer need feel embarrassed about their origin. The region's image has been dramatically transformed, and much of this came about through its music and theater.

Periodical Bibliography

The following articles have been selected to supplement the diverse views presented in this chapter.

Deborah Amos
"Pop Culture Drives Desire for Nose Jobs in Iraq," National Public Radio, October 10, 2005. www.npr.org.

Eleanor Hall
"Beware the One-eyed Monster," *Australian*, October 4, 2006. www.theaustralian.com.au.

Solenn Honorine
"Muslim Pop Culture on the Rise in Indonesia," VOANews.com, April 5, 2010. www1.voanews.com.

Jeremy Lott
"Jesus Sells: What the Christian Culture Industry Tells Us About Secular Society," *Reason*, February 2003. http://reason.com.

Dennis O'Brien
"Going Which Way? Catholicism and Pop Culture," *Commonweal*, September 22, 1995.

Hanna Rosin
"Pop Goes Christianity: The Deep Contradictions of Christian Pop Culture," *Slate*, May 5, 2008. www.slate.com.

Jake Swearingen
"Carl Wilson: Tastes Are Composed of a Thousand Misunderstandings," *Crawdaddy*, February 6, 2009. www.crawdaddy.com.

George Webster
"Brazil's Soap Operas Linked to Dramatic Drop in Birth Rates," CNN.com, September 10, 2009. www.cnn.com.

Catherine Wentworth
"Expat Interview: Jonas Anderson and Christy Gibson," Women Learning Thai . . . And Some Men Too Blog, December 9, 2009. http://womenlearnthai.com.

For Further Discussion

Chapter 1

1. In light of the viewpoint by Monte Reel, do you think that radios play music that is popular, or is popularity determined by what plays on the radio?

2. Andrew Guild argues that American culture's popularity dilutes Australia's culture. Why might Carl Wilson partially disagree with him? Whose argument do you think is more persuasive?

Chapter 2

1. Imagine a European musician who uses extensive sampling in her work and wants to sell her music in China. Based on the viewpoints in this chapter, in what ways would restrictive copyright laws hurt her? In what ways might they help her? Overall, do you think restrictive copyright laws would help or hurt her career?

2. Kevin Donovan argues that China and India would be hurt by stronger intellectual property laws. Based on the discussions by Campbell Smith and Paul Wiedel, do you think that China and India have a moral duty to protect copyright, even if to do so would harm their economies and people? Explain your answer.

Chapter 3

1. Krishna Rau discusses Canadian censorship of homophobic lyrics; Lawrence A. Stanley discusses American censorship of child pornography in comics; Lynette Lee Corporal discusses Thai censorship of a film about child sex slavery. Which, if any, of these forms of censorship do you feel is justified? Explain your reasoning.

Chapter 4

1. Elena Baraban argues that a Russian television show has improved attitudes toward the police. If you could use television to affect the attitudes of your culture, what messages would you put in popular programs? Do you think it is ethical to try to use the media to shape beliefs in this way, even if the outcome is beneficial? Explain your reasoning.

2. Terry Miller argues that Isan music has diminished prejudice toward people in Thailand's Isan region. Does this contradict Louis de Lamare's viewpoint from Chapter 1? Explain your answer.

Organizations to Contact

The editors have compiled the following list of organizations concerned with the issues debated in this book. The descriptions are derived from materials provided by the organizations. All have publications or information available for interested readers. The list was compiled on the date of publication of the present volume; the information provided here may change. Be aware that many organizations take several weeks or longer to respond to inquiries, so allow as much time as possible.

Advanced Cultural Studies Institute of Sweden (ACSIS)
Campus Norrköping, Linköping University
Norrköping, Kungsgatan 38
  SE-601 74
+46 11 36 34 35
Web site: www.isak.liu.se

The Advanced Cultural Studies Institute of Sweden (ACSIS) is an independent unit with Linköping Univesity in Sweden that is devoted to studying interplay between cultural forms, social practices, and institutionalized structures of domination in order to understand how texts, subjects, and contexts interact to reinforce or challenge relations of meaning, identity, and power. It advances its goals through programs for visiting scholars, research, publications, seminars, and conferences. ACSIS publishes the journal *Culture Unbound* and features papers, reports, and articles on its Web site.

Australia Council on Children and the Media (ACCM)
PO Box 447, Glenelg SA   5045
  Australia
+61 8 8376 2111 • fax: +61 8 8376 2122
e-mail: info@youngmedia.org.au
Web site: www.youngmedia.org.au

Australia Council on Children and the Media (ACCM) is a not-for-profit company that provides educational resources and engages in advocacy to encourage families, industry, and decision makers in building and maintaining a media environment that fosters the health, safety, and well-being of Australian children. Its publications include *small screen*, a monthly news review; *Mind over Media* fact sheets available in PDF form; and books and articles available through its Web site. Its site also includes an extensive list of movie reviews.

Canadian Music Creators Coalition (CMCC)

3647 Avenue Henri-Julien, Montreal, Quebec   H2X 3H4
   Canada
e-mail: musiccreators@gmail.com
Web site: www.musiccreators.ca

Canadian Music Creators Coalition (CMCC) is an organization of music creators that advocates on legal and copyright issues, often times in opposition to the stances taken by record companies and music publishers. Its Web site includes position papers, press releases, and news items.

Center for Media Literacy (CML)

23852 Pacific Coast Highway, #472, Malibu, CA   90265
(310) 456-1225 • fax: (310) 456-0020
e-mail: cml@medialit.org
Web site: www.medialit.org

The Center for Media Literacy (CML) seeks to increase critical analysis of the media through its publication of educational materials and Medialit Kits. CML was founded on the belief that media literacy is an essential skill in the twenty-first century, and individuals should be empowered from a young age to make informed choices about the media they consume. *CONNECT!ONS* is the official newsletter of the organization, with archival issues available online. Additional informative materials can be browsed by topic on the CML Web site.

Centre for Popular Culture

Kloveniersburgwal 48, Amsterdam   NL-1012 CX
+31(0)20-525 3680 • fax: +31(0)20-525 3681

e-mail: populaircultuur@fmg.uva.nl
Web site: www2.fmg.uva.nl/populairecultuur/

The Centre for Popular Culture is part of the Department of Communication of the University of Amsterdam. It contributes to the research of the department, focusing on television, video games, popular music, sport, and citizenship. Its Web site includes summaries of ongoing research and links to media reports about the center's work.

Entertainment Software Ratings Board (ESRB)

317 Madison Avenue, 22nd Floor, New York, NY   10017
Web site: www.esrb.org

The Entertainment Software Ratings Board (ESRB) was founded in 1994 to be the self-regulating body for the entertainment gaming industry. The board has been charged with multiple duties including: determining content-based ratings for computer and video games, enforcing advertising guidelines set by the industry, and ensuring online privacy practices for Internet gaming. The ESRB was created to aid all consumers, especially families, in making appropriate decisions about which games to purchase. Additional information about the ratings system and current projects by the ESRB can be read on its Web site.

Film Distributors' Association (FDA)

fax: 020 7734 0912
e-mail: info@fda.uk.net
Web site: www.launchingfilms.com

The Film Distributors' Association (FDA) is the trade body for theatrical film distributors in the United Kingdom. It provides advocacy for film distributors and services for journalists. It publishes *FDA Yearbook*, which includes data on the previous year in British films and illustrated articles on film distribution. The organization also publishes a guide to UK film distribution for students looking to work in the film industry; and *Scoop*, a pocket quarterly magazine containing contacts and information about forthcoming features. FDA's Web site includes film schedules, film data, and information about film piracy.

Focus on the Family

(800) A-FAMILY (232-6459)
Web site: www.focusonthefamily.com

Focus on the Family is a Christian organization dedicated to the promotion of traditional family values, both nationally and internationally. Through a combination of radio and Internet broadcasts, diverse publications, and conferences, Focus on the Family works to inspire married couples worldwide to maintain their families and raise their children according to Christian beliefs. This organization offers writings elucidating its concerns about the value of contemporary pop culture including *The Influence of MTV*, *The Lost Ethics of Pop Culture*, and *Innocence Lost*.

Free Expression Policy Project (FEPP)

170 West Seventy-sixth Street, #301, New York, NY   10023
Web site: www.fepproject.org

With its founding in 2000, the Free Expression Policy Project (FEPP) began work to advocate for free speech, copyright regulation, and media democracy. The organization's work focuses on restrictions on publically funded projects, Internet filters and ratings systems, copyright laws, corporate media consolidation, and censorship. FEPP examines issues relating to the media and popular culture as they are raised, and seeks to provide a balanced assessment of each of these topics of inquiry. The FEPP Web site offers reports and commentary covering issues such as the Internet, media policy, and violence in the media.

Students for Free Culture (SFC)

(585) 506-8865
e-mail: board@freeculture.org
Web site: http://freeculture.org

Students for Free Culture (SFC) is an international chapter-based student organization that promotes the public interest in intellectual property and information and communications technology policy. It has chapters in more than forty schools and universities. SFC's Web site includes a blog with news about free culture issues and links to SFC projects including the nonprofit record label Antenna Alliance and Open University, a campaign to encourage universities to use open networks and free software.

Bibliography of Books

Matthew Allen
and Rumi
Sakamoto
Popular Culture, Globalization and Japan. New York, NY: Routledge, 2006.

Keith Aoki, Jamie
Boyle, Jennifer
Jenkins
Bound by Law?: Tales from the Public Domain. Durham, NC: Duke University Press, 2008.

Peter Blecha
Taboo Tunes: A History of Banned Bands and Censored Songs. San Francisco, CA: Backbeat Books, 2004.

Lane Crothers
Globalization and American Popular Culture, 2nd ed. Lanham, MD: Rowman & Littlefield, 2010.

Michael Drewett
and Martin
Cloonan, eds.
Popular Music Censorship in Africa. Burlington, VT: Ashgate Publishing Company, 2006.

J. Michael Finger
and Philip
Schuler, eds.
Poor People's Knowledge: Promoting Intellectual Property in Developing Countries. Washington, DC: World Bank and Oxford University Press, 2004.

M.T. Kato
From Kung Fu to Hip Hop: Globalization, Revolution, and Popular Culture. Albany, NY: State University of New York Press, 2007.

Jytte Klausen
The Cartoons That Shook the World. New Haven, CT: Yale University Press, 2009.

Lawrence Lessig — *Free Culture: The Nature and the Future of Creativity.* New York, NY: Penguin Books, 2004.

Mark LeVine — *Heavy Metal Islam: Rock, Resistance, and the Struggle for the Soul of Islam.* New York, NY: Three Rivers Press, 2008.

Rini Bhattacharya Mehta and Rajeshwari V. Pandharipande — *Bollywood and Globalization: Indian Popular Cinema, Nation, and Diaspora.* London, UK: Anthem Press, 2010.

Andrew C. Mertha — *The Politics of Piracy: Intellectual Property in Contemporary China.* Ithaca, NY: Cornell University Press, 2005.

Jan Nederveen Pieterse — *Globalization and Culture: Global Mélange,* 2nd ed. Lanham, MD: Rowman & Littlefield, 2009.

Richard Poplak — *The Sheikh's Batmobile: In Pursuit of American Pop Culture in the Muslim World.* Berkeley, CA: Counterpoint, 2010.

Daniel Radosh — *Rapture Ready!: Adventures in the Parallel Universe of Christian Pop Culture.* New York, NY: Scribner, 2008.

Ying Zhu and Christopher Berry, eds. — *TV China.* Bloomington, IN: Indiana University Press, 2009.

Index

Geographic headings and page numbers in **boldface** refer to viewpoints about that country or region.